Paul Stephens

SOCIAL PEDAGOGY
Heart and Head

Paul Stephens

SOCIAL PEDAGOGY
Heart and Head

Studies in Comparative Social Pedagogies and International Social Work
and Social Policy, Vol. XXIV

www.eh-verlag.de

Stephens, Paul

SOCIAL PEDAGOGY Heart and Head

Studies in Comparative Social Pedagogies and International Social Work and Social Policy, Vol. XXIV

Editor of the series: Peter Herrmann

Editorial board : Beatriz Gershenson Aquinsky, Maria Anastasiadis, Christian Aspalter, Torben Bechmann, Nuria Pumar Beltran, Yitzhak Berman, Kezeban Celik, Hsiao-hung Nancy Chen, Geoffrey Cook, Judit Csoba, Leta Dromantiené, Wendy Margaret Earles, Franz Hamburger, Arno Heimgartner, Alpay Hekimler, Peter Herrmann, Sibel Kalaycioglu, Francis Kessler, Jerzy Krzyszkowski, Yeun-wen Ku, Nadia Kutscher, Juhani Laurinkari, Wan-i Lin, Jussara Maria Rosa Mendes, Letlhokwa George Mpedi, Julia O'Connor, M. Ramesh, Mae Shaw, Dorottya Szikra, Stephan Sting, Sven Trygged, Hans van Ewijk, Paul Ward, Luk Zelderloo
www.socialcomparison.org

1. Edition 2013
ISBN: 978-3-86741-830-0
© Europäischer Hochschulverlag GmbH & Co. KG, Bremen, 2013.
www.eh-verlag.de

Dedication

I dedicate this book to Professor Pat Petrie, Professor Chris Kyriacou and Associate Professor Roger Mathiesen. Pat, when I was new to social pedagogy, you introduced me to its secrets and its power for good. Chris, as my knowledge of social pedagogy grew, you enthralled me with your incisive questions and became my Socrates. Roger, you have taught me how important it is to buttress social pedagogic practice with rigorous social pedagogic theory.

Foreword
by Jacob Kornbeck

This aims to be a foreword as well as an endorsement, as indeed, it was with great pleasure and enthusiasm that I accepted Paul Stephens's invitation to write the foreword to this exciting new textbook. I accepted the assignment because I was impressed by this text, which is the first of its kind, and because I am convinced that it will fill a gap.

Social pedagogy is a reality in most European countries: as an occupation or a profession, and/or as an academic discipline in teaching and/or research, yet social pedagogy carries many different names in different national and regional contexts. It is not always visible across the border of nation states, and especially not if literature searches are made in English. Yet this situation is not the dysfunctional representation of an otherwise social pedagogy-friendly reality, but rather the very functional representation of a reality where social pedagogy has been lacking visibility at the European (and indeed global) level, aided as it were by the absence of a social pedagogy tradition in the Anglo-Saxon world.

Now, however, this is changing, as social pedagogy research has been carried out for a few years in the UK and social pedagogy courses at BA and MA level have been set up there. In early 2012, even the USA followed suit with a first MA course. Against the backdrop of a nascent social pedagogy paradigm (in professional and academic contexts), the absence of English-medium social pedagogy literature inevitably becomes something of a problem: both because the Anglophone nations need their own textbooks for teaching social pedagogy (they being far less inclined to use literature in other languages than other linguistic communities may be), and also because English, as the global and European *lingua franca*, is the natural and most functional medium for carrying a social pedagogy discourse across borders: like it or not, there is no substitute to English. But then precisely, the absence of an English-language textbook becomes a major lacuna in professional and academic literature. Social pedagogy cannot do with the books of other disciplines and professions, such as social work, because social pedagogy is a tradition in its own right and needs its own discourse (see AIEJI, 2008).

True, isolated articles can be found in professional and academic journals and in the occasional edited book. An exquisite little collection of edited books has been dedicated specially to explaining, illustrating and discussing social pedagogy, some of them published in England (Cameron & Moss, 2011; Petrie, et al., 2006), others in Germany

(Kornbeck & Rosendal Jensen, 2009, 2011, 2012) and still others in Sweden (Eriksson & Winman, 2010; Gustavsson, Hermansson & Hämäläinen, 2003). Yet attractive, illustrative and informative as they are, these books are not textbooks.

In this unique situation, this book may well be history in the making – academic history, including research and teaching alike – for it seems to me that Paul Stephens has written the first-ever English-language social pedagogy textbook. Just like I felt privileged, 22 years ago, to live in Germany when the Wall came down and the Iron Curtain opened up, so I feel privileged – albeit on a different scale and in a different way – to be an eyewitness of the emergence of a nascent English-language social pedagogy discipline. And such a discipline cannot do with practice-related teaching alone, with curricula and policy papers, not even with a nascent job market for social pedagogy graduates: it needs theory, doctrine and textbooks.

An invited foreword is an opportunity to give credit where credit is due, and Paul Stephens deserves credit for having shown the courage and resolve to write the first textbook and fill the gap.

Paul Stephens deserves credit for having adopted an approach clearly anchored in the humanities, for this is what makes social pedagogy so special, and indeed different from social work.

Finally, and last but not least, Paul Stephens deserves credit for having adopted the life-span perspective, embracing all age groups, instead of repeating the usual simplification of equating social pedagogy merely with certain types of work with children and young people. As such, social pedagogy does not make sense and could just as well be labelled as something else than social pedagogy. But social pedagogy has the potential to provide a conceptual framework for work with all age groups (Böhnisch, [1997] 2008). As one who believes strongly in this way of framing social pedagogy, I am immensely happy that the first English-language textbook should adopt this perspective. It is not least this aspect of the book which I expect will make Paul Stephens's book stand out in the English-speaking world.

I can only express my hope that the book will be discovered and used by those engaged in teaching and researching social pedagogy in all its facets. Writing the first textbook is always a daring endeavour. It takes courage and a belief that this is the right thing to do. And true to the spirit of social pedagogy – this unpredictable, hard-to-catch, humanistic thing with undeniable artistic affinities – I feel tempted to close with a

III

quotation from A.A. Milne's Winnie-the-Pooh: *"Piglet I had decided to catch a heffalump."* We cannot always be sure what the heffalump will look like, but if we are true social pedagogues, we must have the courage to set out looking for it.

Uccle, Brussels, Belgium, September 2012

Jacob Kornbeck

References

AIEJI [International Association of Social Educators / Association Internationale des Educateurs Sociaux] (2008): The Professional Competences of Social Educators: a conceptual framework. (Working document for the AIEJI World Congress, Copenhagen, 4-7 May 2009). http://www.aieji2009.dk/upload/aieji2009/professional%20competences%20of %20social%20educators.pdf

Böhnisch, L. [1997] (2008): Sozialpädagogik der Lebensalter. Weinheim: Juventa Verlag

Cameron, C. & Moss, P. (eds) (2011): Social Pedagogy and Working with Children and Young People: Where Care and Education Meet. London: Jessica Kingsley Publishers

Eriksson, L. & Winman, T. (red.) (2010): Learning to Fly: Social Pedagogy in a Contemporary Society. Göteborg: Daidalos

Gustavsson, A.; Hermansson, H. E. & Hämäläinen, J. (red.) (2003): Perspective and theories in social pedagogy. Göteborg: Daidalos

Kornbeck, J. & Rosendal Jensen, N. (eds) (2009): The Diversity of Social Pedagogy in Europe. Bremen: Europäischer Hochschulverlag (Studien zu vergleichender Sozialpädagogik und internationaler Sozialarbeit und Sozialpolitik, vol. VII)

Kornbeck, J. & Rosendal Jensen, N. (eds) (2011): Social Pedagogy for the Entire Lifespan. Bremen: Europäischer Hochschulverlag (Studien zu vergleichender Sozialpädagogik und internationaler Sozialarbeit und Sozialpolitik, vol. XV)

Kornbeck, J. & Rosendal Jensen, N. (eds) (2012): Social Pedagogy for the Entire Lifespan. Bremen: Europäischer Hochschulverlag (Studien zu vergleichender Sozialpädagogik und internationaler Sozialarbeit und Sozialpolitik, vol. XVIII)

Petrie, P.; Boddy, J.; Cameron, C.; Wigfall, V. & Simon, A. (2006): Working with Children in Care: European Perspectives. Maidenhead: Open University Press/McGraw-Hill

Contents

Acknowledgements

On 1st January 2007, I was appointed to the Inaugural Chair of Social Pedagogy at the University of Stavanger, Norway. I knew a little about the discipline, but mainly as a rose by another name. Over the past five years, I have struggled to excavate the riddles and surprises of social pedagogy, and will continue to do so. Notwithstanding, I have fallen in love with the discipline for the right reason. Social pedagogy is close to my heart because it has taken on a noble project: to place itself in the service of those who have least today so that they may have a better tomorrow.

I owe a great debt to many friends and colleagues without whose help this book would not have been published. Jacob Kornbeck had faith in the project and passed the baton to Professor Peter Herrmann, who decided to publish it. Both are distinguished social pedagogues in their own right, so their endorsement means a lot to me.

Long before I started writing the book, I was beholden to Professor Terje Murberg, who encouraged me to apply to the Inaugural Chair of Social Pedagogy and to Professor Sverre Moe, who appointed me to that position in 2007. Both are eminent scholars in their respective fields, Psychology and Sociology.

Since my appointment, I have worked hard to loosen the kernel of social pedagogy and to make the discipline better known and understood in the Anglophone world. During that period, I have learnt a great deal from Professor Reidar Østerhaug, Professor Kari Søndenå, Associate Professor Roger Mathiesen and my loyal, steadfast friend, Professor Hans-Jørgen Wallin Weihe, all of whom have tutored and sharpened an inquisitive mind.

I must also express my gratitude to the distinguished researchers at the Centre for Understanding Social Pedagogy (CUSP), itself a part of the Thomas Coram Research Unit (TCRU), Institute of Education, University of London. They are helping me to escape the Weberian realm of the vaguely felt in order to understand social pedagogy more fully.

I do not have room to mention all the CUSP members, some of whom are based at TCRU, others not, whose ideas and critique have taught me so much. However, I am particularly grateful to: Heinz Sünker, Claire Cameron, Mark Smith, Bill Whyte, Janet Boddy, David Crimmens, Peter Moss, Filip Coussée, and Valerie Wigfall.

1

Last but not least, as the saying goes, I want to thank my students at the University of Stavanger for giving me the opportunity to test out many earlier drafts of this book in the lecture hall. I hope the benefit has been mutual.

Chapter 1
Introducing social pedagogy

'Deeds uninformed by educated thought can take false directions.'
(Martin Luther King, 1969, p. 150)

Background

I find it wearisome when authors delay defining the subject that they are writing about. So, at the risk of being a little too hasty, here is a succinct and, I believe, broadly accurate definition (or conception) of social pe dagogy:

KEY DEFINITION

'Historically, social pedagogy is based on the belief that you can decisively influence social circumstances through education' (Hämäläinen, 2003, p. 71).

Had I been Hämäläinen, I would have added "and contemporaneously" after 'Historically', but that is a benign quibble. The essential idea is that social learning, whether through teaching or other experiences, increases the potential for agentic action. I should add that even though the above definition is a good start, there are other (usually related) definitions of social pedagogy. I shall consider some of these in due course.

For now, though, I must emphasise that social pedagogy, as a discipline, directs attention to both "the social" and "the pedagogic". In other words, social pedagogic theory-builders draw upon social and educational perspectives, particularly, when these vistas enlighten each other. Illustrative of the point, an "education" into "social skilfulness" involves helping a person to become an educated social navigator. The particular educational or social theory that applies to social pedagogic thinking, depends upon particular contexts. Thus, for example, social cognitive theory is relevant in preparing (or educating) individuals for specific kinds of social interaction.

In this book, I use the terms 'pedagogy' and 'education' as synonyms. It is possible to have a semantic debate about this. However, I have found that, in most cases, both terms signify the same or at least a similar process: that of teaching and learning in a variety of ways. Even so, I have avoided equating 'social education' with 'social pedagogy' for a simple reason. The former term is often used to denote 'moral education' in schools. Yes, social pedagogy embraces this dimension too. However, as a discipline, it is altogether more expansive, encompassing teaching and learning in and outside of school.

KEY DEFINITION

Pedagogy (or education) is a process of teaching and learning in a variety of ways.

At the core of social pedagogy, as in any other social science, is its theory and practice. This is why the two chapters that address theory and practice are lengthier than the chapters that follow. I shall start, though, by taking up a question that is often asked by those who are new to the discipline of social pedagogy: Is it not the same as social work?

Social pedagogy and social work

Like many disciplines, social pedagogy rubs shoulders with kindred spirits, notably, social work. It is therefore important to be clear, as far as this is possible, about the similarities and the differences between social work and social pedagogy. Helpfully, Hämäläinen (1989) has proposed that social pedagogy might be seen as a meta-theory of social work education. Notwithstanding, this begs the question: What is the link between social work and social pedagogy?

Here are four possible answers:

1. There is no link because they are not the same. Social work engages social policy solutions; social pedagogy uses pedagogic solutions.

2. There are tenuous links in that they both study and seek to prevent social problems and promote human wellbeing, but often in quite different ways. Social workers are more inclined to look for by-proxy remedies, while social pedagogues are keen to promote dialogic resolutions.

3. There are strong links because the two disciplines address the task of confronting structural injustice and upholding individual and social justice, acting <u>on behalf of</u> and <u>with</u> oppressed groups.

4. They are essentially the same because social workers and social pedagogues both apply the insights of pedagogic theory (arguably in varying degrees) to the micro- and macro tasks of co-operative enablement for and with oppressed groups; and both tackle the primary causes of social problems in unjust societies.

Back to Hämäläinen's (1989) thought-provoking suggestion that social pedagogy might be seen as a meta-theory of social work education. What he has in mind is a professional education that incorporates the observing and understanding of social problems through social pedagogic spectacles (cf. 2003). I interpret this as a bridge-building idea. Social pedagogy still retains its pedagogic signature, but social workers can – and need to – put on social pedagogic spectacles if they wish to benefit from pedagogic ways of seeing.

By way of practice illustration, a social worker might use her institutional vantage point to acquire a wheelchair for a disabled person, while simultaneously engaging in pedagogic dialogue with the service user regarding the most suitable model. Wheelchair users know a great deal on the practical physics of wheelchair design. This knowledge can be shared with the social worker in order to ensure that an informed choice leads to a design tailored to specific user needs. Such pooling of knowledge breaks down, indeed reverses, conventional "expert-novice" communication, thereby giving credence and respect to user voice. But there are cultural issues to consider. In the UK, for example, there is still a tendency for social workers to decide in advance what the service user's best interest is. By contrast, in Nordic countries, a dialogic approach is rooted in social work culture, particularly, when social pedagogic considerations are part of the story.

It is, of course, one thing to argue the case for a social pedagogic meta-theory of social work and another to find this approach in the real world. In that regard, Herrmann's (2011) identification of a deficit orientation in social work and a developmental orientation in social pedagogy is surely important. In what he admits to be a schematic representation, Herrmann highlights the differences in the form of ideal types (cf. Weber, 1949). The particular context concerns the unemployment of people who experience "mental disabilities" and a migratory background. Note too that Herrmann adds a third category: Social policy.

	Social policy	Social work	Social pedagogy
Aim of activity	Labour market orientation crucial for social integration	Social disadvantage and exclusion orientation; application of medical/ psychological model, with emphasis on support through self-help	Developing the persona and palliating 'conflict boundaries' by nurturing individual potential and achievement
Level of activity	Demand focus (job creation) or supply promotion (employability)	Individual adaptation and/or local solutions. Galvanizing community projects	Personal development, especially through communicative action
Strategy	Economic, regional, development, social welfare & education policies	Labour market qualification programmes & re-integration, as well as community development	Pedagogic development
Actor perspective	Mainly top-down and institutionalist	Partnership (often paternalistic) with individuals & groups, though embedded in an institutional framework	Empowerment of individuals in their settings; can be paternalistic & 'educationalist'; pre-conceived notions of the 'good individual' & the 'good society'

Adapted from Herrmann (2011), Table 2.1, p. 40 (2011)

Herrmann's (2011) recognition that his categories are ideal types, indicates that, dependent on specific contexts, the lines might be fluid and the areas grey. For example, the galvanization of community will, is not unique to social work; it is also found in social pedagogic work (cf., Freire 1996a; Stephens, 2012).

Interestingly, Kornbeck (2012) argues that social pedagogy and social work can be viewed as prominent but distinct sub-categories within a generic category of "social professions". At the same time, he (ibid., p. 14) notes that some commentators see a 'gradual and unavoidable rapprochement' between social pedagogy and social work. In that context, the work of Hans Pfaffenberger in the mid-1960s is of paramount importance, notes Kornbeck. For, 'Pfaffenberger famously introduced the "slash notation" (Schrägstrichnotation) of "social work/social pedagogy" (Sozialarbeit/Sozialpädagogik) and predicted that … social and social pedagogical work must […] be seen and understood as one unitary functional system of societal helping activities.' (ibid, p. 14).

Another perspective is to see social pedagogy as a theoretical basis for multi-profession pedagogic action instead of a special profession. The debate, however, goes on, particularly with regard to the alleged fusion of social work and social pedagogy. For example, in the UK, where social work has a long tradition, social pedagogic thinking and practice is generally considered as fairly new and distinct from social work, being a recent "import" from Continental Europe over the past two decades. Not only that, British politicians, starting with the Blair government, are increasingly looking to countries such as Denmark and Germany in order to learn and incorporate more social pedagogic imagination into UK social care. Whether the final result will be divergence or convergence remains to be seen.

Social pedagogy arrives in the UK

Indeed, the UK has witnessed a rapidly growing interest in Continental European social pedagogy over the past ten years or so (Stephens, 2009; Coussée et al, 2010; Cameron et al, 2011). Some British academics, welfare organisations and social policymakers are contributing to this development. The Centre for Understanding Social Pedagogy (hereafter CUSP) at the Thomas Coram Research Unit (hereafter TCRU), Institute of Education, University of London is playing a prominent role in this venture. For more information, you can visit the CUSP website at:

http://www.ioe.ac.uk/research/40899.html

Professor Pat Petrie, Head of CUSP, is one of the most prolific writers on social pedagogy in the English-Speaking world. She pioneered the search

7

for the roots of the discipline in the history of British childcare. Petrie has also imported aspects of promising social pedagogic practice from Continental Europe into the UK. Furthermore, she is at the forefront of efforts, along with Professor Claire Cameron at Anglia Ruskin University, Cambridge, to make social pedagogy a key subject in the education and training of the British child workforce.

British politicians have recently shown good will by funding a TCRU pilot programme in English children's homes. This involved Continental European social pedagogues working with British staff over a period of two years [2009-2011] (Cameron et al, 2011). In addition, Essex County Council launched a three-year project to introduce social pedagogy into their children's residential services in September 2008 (Hannon et al, 2010). So social pedagogy is on the move in England, a development which is backed by national and local policymakers. The search is on for social care professionals who have studied and practised social pedagogy in Continental Europe and who can model their discipline in the UK (cf. Cameron et al, 2011).

Many of these sought-after professionals come to this country fully qualified in social pedagogy. The problem is that there are not enough of them, neither to mentor the child workforce in England nor to engage in practice themselves. This means that many more social pedagogues will have to be educated in the UK. It is therefore reassuring that courses in social pedagogy are now available in England and Scotland. Hopefully, UK- educated social pedagogues will help to put aside the tired "institutionalisation" that has dominated care in English children's homes. And what will they be able to offer? – warm, confidence-boosting relationships in children's daily settings: at the seaside, on field trips, in after-school clubs and so forth. But there is a challenge. Stated bluntly, there is a general lack of knowledge of social pedagogy in the UK. In particular, social pedagogic theory is seriously understated in many British publications. Indeed, one of the reasons for writing this book is to underscore the signature character of the discipline by extending its lexicon.

Another Achilles' heel in British social pedagogy, which is gradually being remedied, is its relative failure to view the discipline as relevant, and 'Not only for Infants, Orphans and Young People' (Kornbeck & Rosendal Jensen, 2011, p. 1), but for people of all ages. Perhaps "failure" is too harsh a word; "lack of focus" is arguably a fairer appraisal. It is therefore salutary to heed Böhnisch & Schröer (2011, p.16), who make it abundantly clear that, 'The stages of life – childhood, youth, adulthood and old age – are traditionally recognizable as objects of social pedagogical analysis.'

This life stage perspective has, up until quite recently, been eclipsed by a predominantly child-only (and then, children with difficulties) single-mindedness in UK social pedagogy. Even in Norway, which has a considerably longer social pedagogic tradition, there is a tendency to regard social pedagogic practice as virtually synonymous with child welfare practice. Hyperbole granted, adults only seem to appear in the frame there as parents or foster parents of children at risk.

The challenge of theory

Petrie and Cameron (2009) suggest that the English are a pragmatic lot, preferring "Theory Lite" to the real stuff in social pedagogy. Practice is all well and good, but not if it is based on hearsay. So I think that English social pedagogic practice needs a lot more theorising. That way, insightful ideas can be critiqued and tentatively emulated (cf. Petrie & Cameron, 2009). For all that, the search for solid theory is a painstaking journey. The needle in the haystack is, at times, clandestine, and when it is found, the elusive text is usually written in mid-19th and early 20th century German. The result is that a great deal of foundational theory in social pedagogy has been lost, not just in translation, but often in no translation at all.

The temptation is then to toss theories from other social sciences (notably, sociology) into the mixing bowl without further ado. Readers are subsequently left to figure out whether these other theories contribute to the social pedagogic discourse, which they might well legitimately do. But, if so, this needs to be made clear. I am not arguing for inflated subject demarcation, but social pedagogy does offer some distinctive insights – notably, the recognition of the social in the pedagogic and the pedagogic in the social – and these deserve recognition. Notwithstanding, self-styled social pedagogic practice is everywhere to be seen. Indeed, it often appears as though almost any form of caregiver work can be regarded as social pedagogy just by calling it so. Such conceptual haziness gives rise to anecdotal musings and a bewildering hotchpotch of ideas flung around with no regard to theory. Martin Luther King's (1969, p. 150) warning that, 'Deeds uninformed by educated thought can take false directions', is a prescient thought. An under-theorised social pedagogy is a discipline, if it can be called so, without a clear perspective.

Yet there is a deep mine of social pedagogic theory waiting to be dug out. The seam is to be unearthed in historical German texts, as indicated, where the foundations of social pedagogic theory were laid. Once the original theory produced in these seminal works is better understood in the UK, more informed practice in the home nation is sure to follow.

Studying social pedagogy in the UK

If British academics and care professionals are serious about exploring social pedagogic practice, then they must study the discipline properly. Encouragingly, and as already indicated, this is starting to happen. Bachelor degree courses in social pedagogy are now available at Aberdeen University and Liverpool Hope University. There are also master degree courses in social pedagogy at the Institute of Education, University of London and at the University of Winchester. The growing attention to social pedagogy in the UK indicates that the subject has a potentially broad and a large audience. Bearing this in mind, I take heart from the optimistic view of the American pedagogue, Jerome Bruner (1977), that any subject can be taught effectively to anyone provided the pitch is right.

With that ambition in mind, I have written a book about social pedagogy in a fairly direct style while trying hard not to trivialise disciplinary content. Dependent on context, the writing mode varies from down-to-earth to academic. Thus, for example, when considering practical issues, such as the lobbying of social policymakers, I write in a frank, candid fashion. On the other hand, the contemplation of philosophical questions requires, if I may state it so, a more scholarly form of writing. No previous knowledge of social pedagogy is assumed. Pre- and in-service care and health professionals, undergraduates of social welfare, education, psychology and sociology, as well as teachers, lecturers and mentors all constitute potential readers. Even the politicians might want to take a look. Because the social pedagogic workforce contains many different professions, instead of addressing one or more specialities, I provide a broad overview of social pedagogic theory and practice, as well as focusing on the linkage between the two domains.

This Introduction is a long chapter; and for good reason. In it, I seek to provide the reader – and, in particular, the reader who is new to social pedagogy – a fundamental and extensive overview of the discipline. The aim is to give the reader a good, basic understanding of social pedagogy before proceeding to matters of social pedagogic theory, practice, values and so forth.

Origins and development of social pedagogy

Social pedagogy as practice has existed for time immemorial. It was just a rose by another name. Hämäläinen (2003, p. 71) puts this well: 'As a tradition of thought and action, social pedagogy is older than the concept or use of the term "social pedagogy" '. Reminiscent of this, research by Kroll and Bacrach (1986) on the care of sick children in early medieval Europe suggests that a lot of expense and effort went into helping them. It is therefore probable that social pedagogic practice, such as comforting sick children, would have occurred without being called as such. Similarly, Lorenz (2004) has noted that the social work tradition in the Anglophone world already contains many of the same elements found in social pedagogy.

KEY QUESTION

Can you think of further examples in England or other countries where social pedagogy has been practised without being referred to as social pedagogy?

That said, Germany is the ancestral home of social pedagogy in the most candid sense. By this, I mean that the term, "social pedagogy", was coined in that country, conceivably by Karl Mager (1810-1858) in 1844. Sünker and Braches-Chyrek (2009) disagree, however, and give the founder's laurel to Friedrich Diesterweg (1790-1866), a contemporary (and, it seems, a friend) of Mager. Regardless, it appears that Mager wanted to inject a stronger societal dimension into education (Lorenz, 2004). Diesterweg (cited by Günther, 1993, p. 6) also believed that education should have a clear social mission:

'First educate men, before worrying about their professional training or their social class, [because] the proletarian and the peasant should both be educated to become human beings.'

11

KEY QUESTION

What point do you think Diesterweg is trying to get across in the above statement? Consider, in that regard, any relevant social pedagogic ideas.

In the late 19th century, another German thinker, Paul Natorp (1854-1924), explicitly referred to social pedagogy as a means for promoting a culture (that is, a way of life) based on Gemeinschaft (community) values (cf. Lorenz, 2004). With that end in mind, Natorp envisaged the "pedagogisation" of social life in the pursuit of solidarity as a counterpart to self-centredness. While Natorp's vision of solidarity is essentially theoretical and broad-brush, notions of social cohesion in contemporary Continental Europe tend to be more practical and specific. For example, in Nordic countries, policymakers have introduced more accessible built environments with the particular aim of making inclusive solidarity practically possible. Even so, Natorp's Big Idea and emancipatory aim still resonates with the real-world goal of fostering community spirit.

There is a connection here with the ideas presented in a seminal work by the German sociologist, Ferdinand Tönnies (1855-1936): *Gemeinschaft und Gesellschaft* (first published in 1887) [*Community and Civil Society*, 2009]. In his book, Tönnies (2009) contrasts Small Community (Gemeinschaft), bound together by kinship and friendship ties and common values, with Large Society (Gesellschaft), a collection of individuals motivated by self-gain. The contrast between a tightly knit village and an inhospitable metropolis captures the essence of these ideal types. Natorp (1904), who was actually a friend of Tönnies, celebrated the community spirit of Gemeinschaft and lamented the selfishness of Gesellschaft. Community life epitomized Natorp's utopian society in which the wilfulness of individuals would be forged into a co-operative will.

The gist of this sentiment is vividly captured in Martin Luther King's (1964, no pagination) longing for a world in which people have 'learned the simple art of living together as brothers'. The humanitarian role of social pedagogy is also found in the ideas of the German scholar, Herman Nohl (1879-1960), who was a contemporary of Natorp. Nohl, a professor of Philosphy and Pedagogy at Göttingen University, sought to put social pedagogic theory into practice through social help, which he envisaged as a professional educative process based on love and understanding (Hämäläinen, 2003). Although there is some controversy concerning Nohl's position on National Socialism, it has been argued that he was forced into early retirement by the Nazis. Furthermore, he envisaged social pedagogic work as an activity that was above sectional political interests. So an anti-Nazi stance does seem more likely.

By way of summary, Hämäläinen (2003) and Lorenz (2008) have helpfully documented some further milestones in the development of social pedagogic theory. Lorenz notes that "community" was to become the key reference point in the German social policy dimension of social pedagogy. Ominously, he also singles out the Fascist project of attempting to combine state and folk notions of community. This found expression in the Nazis' misuse of social pedagogy, which sought to present the German nation as a racially defined "folk community". Here is a timely reminder that even though social pedagogy originated as a discipline that was deeply engaged in moral argumentation, it cannot be reduced to just one particular moral philosophy. Context counts because culture plays a crucial role in how social pedagogy is conceived and implemented.

Yet, despite the exploitation of the discipline for ignoble political ends, Lorenz (2008) adds that most social professionals, who had not lost their jobs on racist or political grounds, either failed to reflect on the political implications of their Nazified social pedagogic work or enthusiastically backed its ideological content. In Nazi hands, the discipline had become a tool of "racial hygiene", thus abandoning the enlightenment project of civilized and humane edification. Social pedagogy would have to earn and reclaim its honourable reputation in post-war Germany. And, indeed, after the fall of the Third Reich, the Nohlian idea of professional social pedagogy did regain lost ground, and the mantle was taken up by Klaus Mollenhauer (1928-1998) and Hans Thiersch (1935-), both Germans, and regarded as among the most important representatives of modern social pedagogy. In the spirit of Nohl, they developed social pedagogy as an autonomous critical discipline whose goal was social emancipation (Hämäläinen, 2003).

Lorenz (2008) dates the renaissance of the pre-Nazi, humanistic form of social pedagogy in Germany to the late 1960s, when the discipline became a critical rallying point for university academics. The year 1970, witnessed the first degree courses in social pedagogy, and student enrolment in the country sored. Another turning point was the appointment of Mollenhauer to the Chair of General Pedagogy and Social Pedagogy at the University of Göttingen in 1972. Mollenhauer committed social pedagogy to the improvement of the lives of the socially disadvantaged (Lorenz, 2008). His (1983) book, *Vergessene Zusammenhänge: über Kultur und Erziehung [Forgotten Connections: On Culture and Upbringing]* is an important German contribution to social pedagogic theory. Although it has not yet been translated to English in full, Friesen and Saevi (2010, online version) helpfully provide some sample translations. These are available at: http://www.culture-and-upbringing.com/index.php/Main_Page

Mollenhauer (2010, online version, p. 27) argues that a child's early socialisation has much more of an influence than 'individual educational interventions' on upbringing, 'no matter how well planned and structured they may be'. Schooling is often based on pre-defined outcomes and totalitarian motives, as well as canonical assumptions. But for Mollenhauer, the role of the pedagogue is to cultivate the inner life of the child. This positions the child as a self-active learner and also reverberates with those aspects of Bildung that nurture self-development. It should be noted that, in the German language, the process of Bildung is often considered loftier than "mere schooling" because it is seen to cultivate the self and to affirm critical insight, unlike being moulded by teachers and instructors.

Thiersch, briefly mentioned already, is (as was Mollenhauer) influenced by a group of German neo-Marxist intellectuals who, in 1923, founded the Institute of Social Research at Frankfurt University, from which developed a perspective known as the "Frankfurt School" (Hämäläinen, 2003). The main contribution of this "School" is "critical theory", which though it has many strands, is united by an allegiance to emancipatory critique. The aim is to explain and change social arrangements that are oppressive, such as racism and poverty wages. Thiersch (Grunwald & Thiersch, 2009) regards social pedagogy as a liberating discipline pledged to support the socially disadvantaged in their struggle to cope throughout the entire lifespan. He is for social justice and against social oppression and opposes the de-politicisation of social problems and the reduction of social care to social control.

At this juncture, I will conclude my brief excursion into the history of social pedagogy. There is, however, still more to be done in the area, not least, the histories of the discipline in other countries. The good news is that classic social pedagogy texts, most of them German, can still be excavated and scrutinised. If this is done well, contemporary social pedagogic thinking will be greatly enhanced.

14

Social pedagogy today

Today, social pedagogy, as already intimated, is practice-heavy and theory-light, at least in the Anglophone world. Furthermore, lack of clarity about what social pedagogy actually is, has kept the subject in the dark. This state of affairs had led to the pasting together of imprecise ideas. The final mock-up is then presented as social pedagogy. It is therefore crucial to understand the foundational theory that underpins the discipline. It is also necessary to develop new theory. Natorp's (1904) seminal textbook of social pedagogy offers an excellent starting point insofar as original theory is concerned. As for newer ideas, although not explicitly stated in social pedagogic terminology, there is much to be found in the work of the Canadian social cognitive psychologist, Albert Bandura (1925-). He is particularly interested in how individuals and groups and communities can improve their lives through efficacy beliefs.

With regard to individuals, self-efficacy is the term used to denote this personal agentic capacity. When groups and communities are involved, social psychologists speak of collective efficacy. But in both cases, efficacy must be personally or collectively believed in, if desired change is to be accomplished. Otherwise, it remains a latent potential. When self-efficacy is believed in, it is called perceived self-efficacy. When collective efficacy is trusted, it is known as perceived collective efficacy.

KEY DEFINITIONS

- An efficacy belief is an individual's or a group's or a community's belief in their capabilities to produce intended effects by their actions.

- Self-efficacy is an individual's latent potential to produce these actions.

- Collective efficacy is a group's or a community's latent potential to produce these actions.

- Perceived self-efficacy is an individual's belief in her potential to produce these actions.

- Perceived collective efficacy is a group's or a community's belief in their potential to produce these actions.

Interestingly, both Natorp (1904) and Bandura (1997) place great stock in the potential of united effort to change society for the better. This is a call for action on the part of ordinary people to take more control in *their* lives and with their *freely chosen priorities* in mind. Nothing is forced here. Decisions are made through dialogic and democratic consent. This form of communication lies at the heart of social pedagogic practice. To be able to develop a sense of personal or collective agency, people – all people – need to understand that their actions hold the power to transform their personal circumstances.

For present purposes, Slife's (2005, pp. 109-110) simple but elucidatory definition of agency is helpful:

KEY DEFINITION

'Agency is the notion that a person (or other animal) "could have done otherwise," i.e., the person has possibilities and choices. Agency for the qualitative researcher allows for personal responsibility. When a boulder rolls down a mountain, we do not hold it agentively responsible for hitting a hiker because it could not have "behaved" otherwise than it did. We assume that it was governed by natural forces that ultimately reduce to the necessity and determinism of causal laws ...'

At the same time, agency is not evenly distributed in society; some individuals and groups have more of it than others. An important (and an ethical) aim of social pedagogy is therefore to facilitate a more even distribution of agency. For this reason, social pedagogues try to encourage hesitant individuals and groups to experience their innate capacity for change. In practical terms, that can be achieved in a variety of ways, one of which is the setting of cognitive and social learning tasks that lead to mastery experiences. Such exercises rest on a fundamental principle of learning theory. Learning is the process of changing existing understanding and practice by making sense of novel encounters. This involves readjusting to innovative challenges, as, for example, solving a new mastery task.

It consequently makes sense that a discipline with the word "pedagogy" in its title should promote change agency. Placing "social" before "pedagogy", also indicates that the emphasis is usually (but not exclusively) on social learning. Successful strategies for personal change in life, in this case, experiencing achievement rather than failure, often rely on guided mastery (Bandura, 1997). For example, building parenting efficacy through watching and discussing videoed incidents on how to help children learn and manage misbehaviour, can produce good results. The imitation and adaption of parent behaviours that work well and are relatively easy to accomplish by other parents, not only offer potential for improved parent-child interactions, but also an enhanced sense of parental capability.

Some efficacy building tasks are harder to achieve than others, but can still lead to positive outcomes if dependable support is at hand. Giving up smoking illustrates this point. Smokers know that they are damaging their health and, in some cases, jeopardising social relationships. However, many of them harbour nagging doubts about being able to kick the habit. Social pedagogues can assist by educating reluctant smokers to discover and enlist self-efficacy or group efficacy, whichever applies. This helps them to take more control over health decisions. A good starting point would be to affirm their capability of quitting the habit. If the smokers believes that this can be achieved through perceived efficacy), the next step, with social pedagogic support (the enabling of perceived efficacy), is to quit.

In this particular example, speaking with a doctor is sensible because simple guidance from a medical professional makes it more likely that a smoker will stop smoking and still be a non-smoker 12 months later (Stead et al, 2008). Another strategy, also based on sound research (Hajek et al, 2009), is to ask recent smokers to identify and then avoid situations that might tempt them to start smoking again. Eschewing locations where smokers congregate is crucial because it strengthens the resolve to stop smoking. When advice is given, it is important that the social pedagogue or other professional and the smoker reach common agreement through respectful dialogue. Joint deliberation must be the guiding principle here. Dialogic communication lifts the Other's voice, and pacifies, without diminishing, the professional's counsel. This makes it easier for the smoker to make self-affirming decisions.

KEY QUESTION

How would you characterise the difference in social pedagogic work between giving instructions and discussing options?

While social pedagogues do not claim to have discovered the concepts of self-efficacy and perceived self-efficacy, both ideas are of paramount importance in social pedagogy (cf. Böhnisch & Schröer, 2011). There is a lesson here. Social pedagogy, like most (if not all) academic subjects, borrows from the theoretical insights of other fields of knowledge. This is not filching, but simply the judicious application of inter-disciplinary knowledge to social pedagogic thinking.

So far, I have briefly introduced the reader to social pedagogic theorising and practising in different contexts. Now it is time to be clearer about what social pedagogy stands for in general terms.

What is social pedagogy?

Social pedagogy is a subject and a practice that formulates and applies pedagogic solutions to social problems. It has a preventative role as well because it seeks to prevent these problems from arising in the first place. Hämäläinen (2005, p. 149) makes the point forcefully:

'Social pedagogical work does not limit itself to problem solving, only. Its professional function is also to maintain well-being and the standard of living. From this function, social pedagogical work acquires its strongly preventive meaning and contents.'

The preventative function of social pedagogy is often eclipsed in the literature because "crisis social pedagogy" looms large. Yes, most of the time, social pedagogues do deal with people in varying degrees of distress. But the nurturing of positive psycho-social climates is also an important aspect of social pedagogic work. Actually, in Norway, social pedagogues are sometimes called milieu therapists or milieu workers. Thus, for example, social pedagogic work in after-school clubs – hugely popular in Norway – aims to nurture pro-social, co-operative relationships among young people, irrespective of the problems they might have or not. The idea is that an affable environment "censors" anti-social behaviour and "rewards" amiable interaction.

There are many examples that illustrate pre-emptive and pro-active aspects of social pedagogic work; for example:

- Providing personal assistance to a child with physical difficulties in order to extend his opportunities for engaging in mainstream events.

- Implementing an anti-school bullying programme in order to foster kinder values in school, thereby hindering the development of aggressive behaviour.

- Providing a young mother with parental guidance on how to relate to an aggressive child.

- Supporting a recovering substance user to develop social skills that will help her to cope with the demands of daily life.

- Petitioning policymakers to prevent high unemployment through investing substantially in education and training.

While the above examples largely deal with social pedagogic practice as a "doing-*for*-others" discipline, that is only (and quite often a small) part of the story. Shifting unjust social structures clearly requires collective muscle and determined lobbyists, but social pedagogy also operates, crucial this, on the micro-level of inter-personal relationships. The famous Brazilian pedagogue, Paolo Freire (1996b), who is generally regarded *de facto* as a social pedagogue, understood that point.

Even though he acknowledged the hard-to-remove structural origins of social suffering, Freire knew that much could be done to help oppressed individuals in the daily round. The key to his emancipatory pedagogy was dialogic relationship, which is conveyed in the notion of "walking alongside" the Other, even "holding their hand". At the same time, Freire (1996b, p. 127) explicitly stated that the role of the "teacher" and the "learner" are, and must be different:

> ' [T]he second basic principle [of educational practice] is the existence of subjects, educators and learners, which does not mean they are equal to each other. The fact that both are subjects of the practice does not nullify the specific role of each one. The former are subjects of the act of teaching; the latter are subjects of the act of learning. The former learn as they teach; the latter teach as they learn.'

It would be impossible to conceive of teaching and learning as activities that do not involve teachers (cf. Shim, 2008). At the same time, Freire's (1996b) relational model positions the teacher and the students as subjects, and, moreover, as subjects who both have something to give and to gain. This expresses an ethical ideal of the social pedagogic relationship: bi-lateral and dialogic, with both parties teaching and learning from each other. For all that, there comes a time, and I think Freire recognises this, when teachers have to teach and learners have to learn. The argument is eloquently expressed by the radical American educationist and friend of Freire, Jonathan Kozol (1993, p. 112), who asserts that too many idealistic teachers, 'speak of themselves as if they were not teachers any longer, but some sort of "incidental person" who just happens to be present among children in the school.'

KEY QUESTION

How do you respond to the assertion below?:

There comes a time when teachers have to teach and learners have to learn.

This is not to propose that teaching should be based on monologue. Interaction between teacher and learner, in those respective but temporal roles, is crucial. In emancipatory social pedagogy, the predominant form of interaction is democratic and dialogic, with a strong focus on joint problem-solving. Even though the teacher often poses the problem, she and the student critically and intelligently explore it together. The idea of holding the Other's hand, 'The Moral Party of Two' (cf. Bauman, 2009, p. 82), implies a mutual act, but more often than not the teacher takes the lead. The aim is to help the learner to "read" and navigate the social world in ways that produce beneficial outcomes: a better understanding of mathematics; a kinder disposition to the victims of bullying; a stronger sense of personal efficacy; and so forth. Moreover, the helping hand is gently released when confident distance takes over from dependent proximity. If such were not so, the learner would become over-reliant on the social pedagogue instead of being able to make brave forays from the nest, knowing all the while that a warm welcome awaits on return.

KEY TASK

Imagine or consider a real social pedagogic relationship. Describe and explain it to someone who has never heard of social pedagogy before.

In order to understand a discipline properly, it is important to consider its subject-specific "signature". That lies in its appellation, which in the present case is social pedagogy. I have done this to some extent, but more needs to be said about the two words that, when used together, give social pedagogy its unique character. The words are "social" and "pedagogy". The original Latin meaning for "social", when used as an adjective (in Latin, "socialisis"), is, "united". In sociology, "social" defines a sense of a minimal degree of solidarity that links human beings together and makes it impossible to ignore each other. In all societies, there are certain common values and norms. These are, to a greater or lesser extent, passed from one generation to another, which assures varying degrees of unity and continuity of collective life (cf. Durkheim, 1994). Nevertheless, "The Social" varies historically and cross-culturally. In short the "The" denotes social specificity.

The project of social pedagogy, based on its foundational origins, is to preserve or, as appropriate, to reinvigorate social solidarity in a way that "predisposes us without difficulty to devotion and sacrifice" (Durkheim, 1994, p. 107) in our relationship with each other. In addition, as Herrmann and van der Maesen (2008) imply, "The social", understood from a participatory angle, is a product of the dialectic interaction between actors and their constructed environment, which has, to an extent already been constructed by other actors. Turning to the word, "pedagogy", the original Greek meaning for this term when used as a noun (in Greek, "παιδαγωγία", or, in the Roman alphabet, "paidagōgiā") is, "the education of children". There is some debate about whether in ancient times the Greeks also used "pedagogy" to include the education of adults. These days, "pedagogy" applies to education in general, irrespective of the learner's age. Placed together, "social" and "pedagogy", from a social pedagogic standpoint, signify learning how to live co-operatively with each other. It is also pertinent to mention that the Latin word for education is "educationem", which originally denoted an education or socialisation into social codes. This intimates that education involves upbringing at home as well as subject-learning in schools. The learning of social values and norms starts in early childhood, with observation and imitation playing a central role.

For example, a child watches her parents comforting a baby brother and then cuddles a baby doll. This kind of learning is often based on replicating the observed behaviour of trusted adult carers, even though young children also learn in others ways: for example, through story-telling, through play and so forth. That said, there is not enough time in life for children to base all their learning on personal guided discovery. For, as the American educational philosopher, Mortimore J. Adler (1987, p.168), makes clear, even though teaching is a cooperative art, 'most human beings need instruction to learn what they could have learned by discovering it for themselves'.

The difference between subject learning and social learning is that the former relies substantially on cognitive (or rational) processes and the latter on affective (or emotional) processes. Put simply, subject learning involves the "head" and social learning involves the "heart". Actually, social pedagogues are interested in head (academic/instrumental learning), heart (social/moral learning) and, along the way, hands (practical learning). However, their speciality is the heart.

Living in harmony

The primary mission of social pedagogy, as originally formulated by Natorp (1904), was, and still is, to serve the common good. This requires nothing less than moral transformation. In the Natorpian paradigm, unencumbered self-interest would yield to mutually dependent solidarity, with social pedagogic thinking and practice as the prime mover. This remaking of society would become the new spirit of the age, leading to, 'a benign regime sworn to the pursuit of universal happiness ...' (Bauman, 2009, p. 197). The envisaged utopia would culminate in a last stand, with Gemeinschaft (community living) facing down and triumphing over Gesellschaft (individualistic living). That, at least, was the dream.

KEY QUESTION

Is it realistic for social pedagogues, such as Paul Natorp, to pursue a dream of a society in which human beings are willing and able to live together in harmony?

Along the way, reason (head) and affect (heart) would have to work in concert, so that rational policymaking would be at the behest of moral vision. The "heart", which as indicated, has a special place in social pedagogic practice, is a complex metaphor. It not only learns, it feels. If values and norms were simply the product of instrumental teaching, there would be something missing. That something is moral conviction, which is emotionally felt rather than rationally worked out. Yet at the same time, the head knows that the conviction is right. For all that, right cannot be "taught" in a classroom. When, for example, a kind heart inspires benevolent action, this is not simply a product of learning.

Consider the following situation. Two people give money to a homeless beggar. The first person has learnt, in a rational sense, that generosity is a socially approved value. He helps the beggar out of a desire to be seen to conform. The second person also knows that generosity is a widely held value, but she gives out of felt compassion for the beggar. This kindness comes from large-heartedness, not from the tactical logic of the head. The beggar's pain is her pain and his joy is vicariously felt. Her action and his relief are emphatic examples of living in harmony.

The example illustrates Mortimer J. Adler's (1941) point – and, with it, Plato's and Aristotle's (in the case of the latter, with the exception of intellectual virtue) – that while the intellectual is teachable, the moral is not. Essentially, moral feelings arise from the conscience, not the chalkboard. They are habituated (both generating and stabilising the conscience) rather than tutored. Moral actions are, in turn, the carriers of acceptable social values. While values vary from situation to situation, most societies share core moral beliefs (values) about right actions (norms). A compassionate disposition and kind action are particularly important. Kindness originally meant kinship or sameness, but it goes by many names today (Phillips & Taylor, 2009). For example, humanity, compassion, open-heartedness and generosity all convey the essence of kindness. At the root of this virtue, is, 'the sympathetic expansiveness linking self to other' (Phillips & Taylor, 2009, p. 4).

What Phillips and Taylor (2009) mean, is that kindness shows itself through a benevolent concern for others and signals a sense of solidarity with them. It would be hard to contemplate a more important value than compassion in the social pedagogic professions. For the main role of the social pedagogue is to help people in need, to offer support that draws on generosity. This intentional susceptibility to 'the Other' (after Levinas's '*l'autre*', 1991) shows the importance attached to *caritas* (or neighbourly love) in social pedagogic ethics. That can express itself in the welcome given to the face of 'the personal Other' (after Levinas's '*le visage d'autrui*', 1991), namely, to the person in need of help.

Caritas also desires that the human being who is being helped, will be able to discover her self-efficacy and act on it in a constructive way. By creating opportunities for those beset by self-doubt to gain a measure of control over their problems, social pedagogues chip away at hesitation and bolster self-belief. In this regard, the experience of success is powerful fuel. It represents a disconfirmation of a morbid fear of failure, a state often habituated through unsupportive socialisation, such as constantly being ridiculed by peers and even family members.

Socialisation

Beginning at infancy and continuing through life, individuals are initiated into society. Sociologists call this process "socialisation". Essentially, socialisation involves two main processes, as illustrated in the following KEY DEFINITION:

KEY DEFINITION

1. The internalisation (taking in and habituation) of values and norms from life experiences in general; this does not require teaching, but rather an affective affinity

2. Being educated in a broad sense: formal/informal; schooled/non-schooled

---

Social pedagogic work is enhanced and limited, in varying degrees, by the way children experience socialisation. Parents whose own caring behaviour is appreciated by their children, engage in social interactions that foster and consolidate kindness. Social pedagogic practice in schools (common in Norway, for example) then takes on a "preventative function" through the nurturing of altruism and the assuaging of self-centred behaviour. On the other hand, if socialisation at home stifles affability, this poses a social pedagogic challenge. The main goal then is to help egocentric children to understand and act on the moral principle of showing consideration for others. This "interventionist role" might sound rather sinister, evoking perhaps, the notion that social pedagogues are the puppet masters of upbringing.

It is important, though, to correct this misunderstanding. To "socialise", even to "re-socialise", are neither complete nor unilateral projects. Social pedagogues must respect individual choice, provided this does not diminish the human dignity of others. Along the journey, so-called "agents of socialisation" can, at times, offer opportunities for children to interact with peers and adults in settings that are known to produce favourable sequels. For example, research shows that positive interaction between different ethnic groups cultivates inter-ethnic tolerance (Allport, 1979). This is to be applauded because racist attitudes have no place in a just society.

If not habituated early, helping children to become attuned to the needs of people around them gets harder with age. Therefore it is important that the receiving and giving of compassion constitute a natural part of the early life course. In that manner, pro-social ways of thinking and acting are more likely to become deeply seated in the child's habitus. In the very early years, some psychoanalysts see this process as the dismantling of infantile illusions of omnipotence. If such misconceptions are deeply etched in the child's psyche, feelings of self-importance can continue into adolescence and adulthood. Lack of empathy can also manifest itself in bullying, namely, unprovoked aggression towards persons who find it hard to defend themselves. The older the bully, the more his aggressive behaviour is likely to persist even if others try to change it (Stephens, 2011a).

KEY DEFINITION

Bullying is unprovoked aggression (psychological, social or physical) over time by one or more persons towards one or more other persons who find it difficult to defend themselves. In short, the harassment is persistent, and there is a power imbalance in favour of the bullies.

On the subject of bullying, it is pertinent to look at two internationally renowned anti-school bullying programmes, each of them based on social pedagogic principles. These are the Olweus Programme Against Bullying and Antisocial Behaviour, developed by Dan Olweus (2001) at Bergen University, and the Zero Programme, developed by Erling Roland (Roland, & Sørensen Vaaland, 2003) at Stavanger University. Both programmes receive backing and funding from the Norwegian government, and, crucially, both have been found to reduce bullying problems in schools (Stephens, 2011a).

While the Olweus and Zero initiatives contain some different approaches, the two programme developers place great stock on rallying pro-social bystander behaviour. Many bystanders try not to get involved in bullying incidents, considering it not their business or worse still, a spectator sport (cf. Smith & Shu, 2000; Salmivalli et al, 2004). If bystanders can be persuaded to speak out against bullying, this could mobilise a considerable amount of latent moral force within the majority. That said, would-be protectors must believe that they can succeed in helping victims of bullying and must avoid putting themselves in danger.

There are two social pedagogic challenges here. One is to unlock the potential of helping behaviour; the other is to increase perceived collective efficacy among the protectors. Olweus uses role-play and the viewing of staged bullying incidents (on video) in order to foster sympathetic understanding of the victim's pain and predicament. Roland recommends the use of student patrols during school recess as an adjunct to adult supervision. Students on patrol are encouraged to wear official, brightly coloured vests in order to enhance their authority and visibility.

KEY TASK

Suggest a practical social pedagogic initiative that a school might try out in an anti-bullying programme. Indicate in what respect social pedagogic thinking underlies your idea.

As said, bullying and other forms of anti-social behaviour respond best to an early response, so pre-schools and primary schools are obvious sites for anti-bullying initiatives, as are family homes where certain parenting practices appear to induce childhood aggression. A research study from Canada (Thomas, 2004), for example, has confirmed previous findings that harsh, punitive parenting is linked to child aggression. Interestingly, however, the study found that some children whose early parenting (when they were at age 2 to 3 years) had been punitive but whose environment became less so at age 8 to 9 years, scored as low in aggressive behaviour as children whose parenting was not punitive at both ages. This suggests that change in parenting behaviour predicts change in childhood behaviour, in both cases for the good.

For all that, some unfortunate habits are more intractable. When people repeatedly compromise others' human rights, social pedagogues have to focus more on protecting potential victims than on trying to change the abusive and aggressive behaviour of perpetrators. Thus, for example, if parents abuse their children, social pedagogues who work in Child Services have a moral (and, probably in most cases, a legal) duty to place the children in safe care – in a foster family, for instance. In anti-school bullying programmes, efforts to change the bully's ways are supplemented with adult surveillance, especially in high risk areas, such as changing rooms.

If children are encouraged to act aggressively, they tend to behave tactically by feigning compliance when it suits their purpose. In contrast, those who are assisted to act fairly for the sake of fairness itself, usually act charitably because this is the right thing to do (Beugre, 2010). Parents whose own behaviour sets a good example can become exceptional role models for their young children. Varying degrees of humane correction, especially with regard to boundary setting, usually play a part in bringing up children too. Being an adult significant other in a child's life, either as a parent or a social pedagogue, demands the sincere modelling of appropriate behaviour. Then, action really will count more than words.

What social pedagogues do

To reiterate an important point, social pedagogues apply pedagogic solutions to social problems. In addition, they seek to prevent social problems from arising in the first place. If and how they achieve these objectives, depends on their professional skills, a person's readiness to change unhelpful habits, structural opportunities and constraints, and so forth. Finding social pedagogic solutions on the personal level requires dialogue, not diktat. Social pedagogues do not want to be in charge. They want to put the other person in charge. To achieve this, it is necessary that both parties, through a respectful exchange of ideas, are able to agree upon a remedy that is enabling rather than directive. To enable, is to make possible; in this case, to make it possible for someone to change a difficult life situation.

In their role as care professionals, where they are often employed in social services, social pedagogues become agents of socialisation. It should be added here that the majority of people who receive social pedagogic support are service users. The services vary and can include: child and youth psychiatry; child welfare; educational psychology; centres for substance users; prison education; schools; care homes; personal assistant provision; community oganisations; and much more. That explains why the term, "service user", is quite frequently used in this book.

The role of the social pedagogue carries the responsibility of helping people to help themselves. Discharging this duty, however, does not involve the peddling of self-help adages. The point is to educate service users to trust in their capacity, with the necessary support, to surmount social problems (cf. NOU, 2009). Quite often, this involves assisting people to change unhelpful behaviours. Moral judgment is not the issue. The aim is to help people, with their co-operation and consent, to alter certain aspects of their lives in ways that bring benefits. The process typically involves gentle conversation between the social pedagogue and the other person. This form of communication brings out the best in social pedagogic practice. It establishes a climate of goodwill in which the two parties can work together to identify challenges and implement remedies.

KEY QUESTION

What is the difference between telling vulnerable people to stand on their own feet and leaving them to it, as opposed to helping them to discover their own feet whilst supporting their endeavor to bring about intended and beneficial consequences?

Although each person has a different role, there is nevertheless an exchange of ideas rather than top-down commands. In the language of sociology, people talk to each other "horizontally" (on a level plane) rather than "vertically" (from unequal positions). Horizontal communication is commonly used in social pedagogic work, a point I shall address in Chapter 5. Helping downhearted people to develop positive, self-affirming habits usually requires professional support. This often takes the form of 'scaffolding' (cf. Bruner, 1996), namely, providing pedagogic props to help the learner to get to the next level. As the learner progresses from a "walk" to a "jog", the social pedagogue removes a bit of the scaffolding. This helps the learner to obtain more personal control over the task. It also increases the chance of accomplishment and reduces the risk of failure.

Actually, failure is really not an option in initial assignments because it can destabilise a protégé's confidence. It is therefore crucial that social pedagogues and service users agree on reachable targets. This echoes the important pedagogic principle that task setting should be approximately matched to a person's capability. I say "approximately", because it is prudent to prospectively expect and stimulate a little extra from the learner. The Russian pedagogue, Lev. S. Vygotsky [1896-1934] (1978, p. 89), conveys this message succinctly: '[T]he only "good learning" is that which is in advance of development.' As the learner makes progress, tasks need to become more challenging. This means that some failures are inevitable. Insecure learners sometimes develop task avoidance strategies if they fall short by refusing to engage future challenges. The social pedagogue should therefore explain that mastery requires persistent effort and that a realistic challenge often carries a "50-50 chance" of success.

The implication is clear. Trying hard is likely to produce both success and failure. The message is also clear. Rejoice in the former and accept the latter as a normal event. If graded tasks do not produce desired results, adjustments in the form of more manageable exercises and extra support offer a first-line approach to the problem. But social pedagogues need to appreciate that some events will be well beyond a person's control. In such cases, it is best if the person gives proxy control to the professional carer. What this means, is that the social pedagogue works on behalf of the individual by navigating social structure with expert eyes.

KEY TASK

Provide a few examples, real or imagined, of circumstances when it might be appropriate for a social pedagogue to act on behalf of another human being by proxy. Justify your conclusions.

That might be seen as a retrograde step. However, if it does not happen too often, it can be a helpful and a necessary strategy, particularly in acute crises. After all, everyone gives proxy control to somebody else on occasion. This might be part of an ordinary routine, as for example, giving a doctor permission to provide medical care. On the other hand, some people habitually give proxy control to others because they do not trust their own self-efficacy. This is a problem that requires social pedagogic guidance in order to tackle unnecessary timidity.

As will have been noted, social pedagogic practice involves educational counselling and social support. Schools should play a role here, but some teachers prefer to see themselves as "educators" rather than "social workers". This perspective represents a narrow and an artificial demarcation of roles. In social pedagogy, however, it is widely understood that the social and the educational infiltrate each other and that social pedagogic work necessarily addresses both elements.

Uniting the social and the pedagogic

Social pedagogic practice occurs at the suture of social care and educational guidance. Cameron (2004, p. 133) makes this point when she argues that, 'Social pedagogy is a professional field that crosses the social work/education divide.' She (2004, pp. 133-134) adds that social pedagogy, 'combines academic training with the development of personal and practical skills and is applicable to work with children and young people and in some cases to work with adults and elderly people as well.' Many of these individuals suffer social disadvantages of one kind or another. Social pedagogues are on their side. The aim is to help them to gain more control over their lives so that they can find different and better ways of coping and, crucially, thriving. Social pedagogic practice aspires to much more than a condition of mere existence. Even those who have less hardship in life can benefit from the work that social pedagogues do. For example, children and young people in general gain much from a positive social climate at school.

When school is friendly and supportive, pupils and teachers are more likely to be up-beat and confident. This is why school social pedagogues strive to develop caring, helping behaviours. In that setting, whole school approaches focusing on altruistic norms are likely to produce the best results because they cultivate common purpose. In concrete terms, much of the work can be done if teachers support students emotionally and socially. The upshot is a secure classroom, where pupils feel safe and wanted (cf. Bru et al, 2002; Stephens, 2011a). Good schools recognise the responsibility they have in nurturing an inclusive climate. This necessitates upholding and praising kind and co-operative behaviour among students and setting clear boundaries about what is unacceptable (e.g. bullying, sexism and racism). Often teachers attend to this "social curriculum" in and outside the classroom. Additionally, some schools employ social pedagogues to provide co-ordination and guidance.

Cameron's (2004) reference to social pedagogic work with adults is also significant. It is a reminder that social pedagogues work with people through the entire lifespan. For example, some social pedagogues support adults who have severe disabilities. Such problems range from complex health needs to serious autistic disorders. In the case of autistic adults, a key task is to assist them to develop improved communication and other social skills. With regard to social pedagogic work with older people, the UK initiative, Befriending of Older Adults, contains many effective measures (Knapp et al, 2011). These include the promotion of social inclusion and efforts to reduce loneliness and depression. The befriender gains too, notably from the personal satisfaction of providing support to a needy human being. As well as enabling people to overcome specific problems, another goal of social pedagogy is to improve society in general, thereby reducing or even eliminating social problems (Sünker & Braches-Chyrek, 2009).

Changing unjust social structures

How can social pedagogues change structural arrangements in society that perpetuate social suffering? They can start by looking behind the statistics on social problems in order to observe visceral suffering at close quarters. Bourdieu's (1999, p. 629) famous narratives of how society is experienced by people who bear, 'the poverty and the "passive violence" of economic and social structures', as well as, 'all the small privations and muted violence of everyday life', make for close reading. True, social policymakers take a keen interest in social statistics, and this is necessary.

How else, for example, would it be possible to measure the level of poverty, racism, bullying and so on without a number? But there is a text too, and it has a name: the service user's voice. It is hard to put a number on the right to be heard, so social pedagogues need to find that voice, listen to it and embrace it in dialogue. They must also bring the concerns of subjugated people into the corridors of political power. In that way, politicians can make policy choices that take account of both "number" and "text".

Social pedagogues have an ethical (and, increasingly, a political) mandate to challenge and correct institutional conditions in society that perpetuate human suffering. When they encounter injustice – for example, lack of regular, affordable public transport in a poor neighbourhood – much can be done by helping individuals and families to solve the problem through collective effort, backed up by professional support. Because many social pedagogues are ambulant care professionals, they often work in the daily environment of the people who need help. This offers many opportunities for face-to-face, outreach initiatives. The possibilities are many and include:

- Neighbourhood canvassing to identify community problems and needs

- Community building strategies with local neighbourhood associations

- Educational, training and life skills programmes for poor immigrants

- Mobile services for sex workers and rough sleepers

- Bringing media attention, with their consent, to the plight of the socially disadvantaged

- Pro-bono legal advice on issues concerning citizens' rights

Engaging in community work can take many forms. Kloppenburg & Hendriks (2010), identify three main models:

1. Support Model – standing alongside people in need and seeking solutions for and with them

2. Catching Clients Model – being on the look-out for needy people and putting them in touch with appropriate services and charities

3. Options & Sanctions Model – using varying degrees of pressure that involve options and sometimes sanctions in order to tackle problems

In order to illustrate two of these models in a real context, I actually use the Support Model and the Catching Clients Model in social pedagogic outreach work with poor Romanians (most of them Roma) in Stavanger, Norway. This is where I live and work. Many of these immigrants beg, play music or sell flowers in the city centre. I become acquainted with them (quite a few speak Italian, as do I, which helps) and find out how I can help. This might be offering a bed for the night (or longer), distributing left-over but fresh food from a soup kitchen where I work as a volunteer, helping out with money problems, enrolling people on Norwegian language courses, providing over the counter medication, organising access to medical and dental care, and, above all, assisting with the paperwork that leads to a permanent ID number and entry into legal employment.

Sometimes I simply come across Romanian beggars and have a chat. At other times, they approach me, often I suspect through word-of-mouth. There is an element of what researchers call "snowballing" here, but my primary objective is social pedagogic advocacy, not academic research. There is also, as indicated, a mixture of "catching" and "support" in the work I do. For example, I "catch" needy Romanians and "support" them by doing the paperwork that can lead to legal residency and employment in Norway. This is an example of social pedagogic work by proxy. A good deal of my time involves steering through the complex bureaucracy involved in applying for the documents that can make this happen. Based on my anecdotal, hands-on experience, I have found that applications are often stymied by having to do the rounds from one civic office to the next – the police, the tax office, social services and so forth. Why not, I thought, do all the paperwork under one roof? I subsequently raised this issue in the local media, and a local Labour Party councillor invited me to meet him. I proposed that there should be a "one-stop-shop" for immigrant job seekers in the city. He agreed and so did City Hall. The result is that there is now a service centre for immigrant job-seekers in Stavanger, where the necessary paperwork can be expedited in one building. I have found that getting the attention of the politicians and, even more importantly, persuading them to enact enabling measures, can add leverage to social pedagogic practice.

KEY TASK

At a recent conference in London when I presented some research findings from my work as a street social pedagogue, it was suggested that I was more of a philanthropist than a social pedagogue. What do you think?

Aim and outline of the book

The aim of this book is to provide an introduction to social pedagogy. A related objective is to identify the defining characteristics of the discipline. Too many writers use the term "social pedagogy" uncritically. For example, you will often read that social pedagogy is holistic, which it is actually. But so too is social work, teaching, and nursing. So being holistic is not the defining feature of social pedagogy because other disciplines use holistic methods as well. Now that you have read **Chapter 1** (Introducing social pedagogy; the aim, I should add, being to provide the beginning reader of social pedagogy with a sure footing), **Chapter 2, Social pedagogic theory**, examines the theoretical underpinning of the discipline. It takes as its starting point the seminal theory of Paul Natorp (1904), who is regarded as a Founding Father of social pedagogy. The chapter examines and explains Natorp's theory and considers how it might be supplemented with contemporary social pedagogic ideas. Out of this mix, and with the addition of some up-to-date ideas of my own, I seek to develop a more coherent theory of social pedagogy for today.

Theory is the cornerstone of any social scientific discipline, and social pedagogy is no exception. It offers clarity of conceptual thinking and a surer footing for best social pedagogic practice. Theory also promotes meaningful dialogue between practitioners, helping each to understand the other. Becoming better acquainted with social pedagogic theory is a necessary but an incomplete project, especially in the UK. New and sharper concepts must be developed if social pedagogy is to escape from what Weber (1949, p. 94) describes as, 'the realm of the vaguely "felt"'.

Chapter 3, Social pedagogic practice, investigates the work that social pedagogues do. It takes up and expands on some of the social pedagogic practices that have been mentioned in this introductory chapter, such as linking theoretical ideas to the practice field. The main aim of the chapter is to provide a generative guide to informed thinking when working as a social pedagogue. This might involve, for instance, acting on a fundamental principle (e.g. "United we stand") and then applying the principle concretely (e.g. helping to set up a community association to promote the rights of lone parents and their children).

Chapter 4, Social pedagogic values, follows that ethical ingress by documenting and evaluating social pedagogic values, both historically and contemporaneously. A brief look at the education of social pedagogues in Norway, where social pedagogy is well established, offers a useful backdrop. The central argument is that compassionate social pedagogy – e.g., the Nordic kind – brings dignity to human life.

Chapter 5, Social pedagogic communication, mainly addresses the dialogic nature of conversations between social pedagogues and service users. The author argues that good practice should, in most cases, be based on horizontal communication. There are times, however, when social pedagogues have to resort to vertical communication. This can occur, for example, when a social pedagogue makes a professional decision in the best interest of a child even if a parent contests it.

Chapter 6, Cross-national lesson-drawing, examines the potential for learning from relevant social pedagogic practice abroad. Kornbeck (2006) rightly warns that the uncritical importing of social pedagogy is unwise. Even so, Rose (2001) is surely convincing in his claim that it makes good sense to explore practice in countries that have done a lot of work and gained valuable experience in a particular field. UK policymakers and social service administrators can learn a lot by selecting what looks to be promising social pedagogic practice abroad and then trying it out in the home country.

Finally, **Chapter 7, Conclusion**, provides a summary of main themes and issues and considers future possibilities for informed and just social pedagogic thinking and practice.

Chapter 2
Social pedagogic theory

'There is nothing so practical as a good theory' (Kurt Lewin, 1951, p. 169)

Introduction

KEY QUESTION

What do you think Kurt Lewin (1951) means when he claims that, *'There is nothing so practical as a good theory'*?

In this chapter, I look at social pedagogic theory, which constitutes the systematic thinking behind social pedagogic practice. In that sense, theory functions as a kind of "simulator" in which ideas can be rehearsed before taking action. Often, the origins of a theory can be traced back to intelligent hunches based on problem-solving efforts in the real world. An "I wonder if this might work" idea could provide the starting point for a new theory. For example, a social pedagogue might have a hunch about how to help an unemployed person who, on her own volition, wants to return to work. Let us assume that the theoretical conjecture is as follows:

A short course based on graded tasks is likely to strengthen the service user's confidence in her ability to ease back into employment at her own pace, and she will do so successfully.

The next step, in consultation and with the consent of the job-seeker, is to enrol her on an appropriate course. Let us assume that the results are good and she finds a job and makes good progress. The social pedagogue has thus found that the idea actually works. This is the start of theory-building. In the example given, the theory (or strictly speaking, the hypothesis) might be formulated in this way:

Guided mastery can help <u>this</u> unemployed job-seeker to find work and to perform well.

Now it is time to try out the theory with other people who are in similar circumstances. If the outcomes are consistently positive, then the theory has gained some credence. Such theory-building has its limits, though, because in this example the idea has only been tried out and found to work with one individual. Yet there are some established theories readily available that have a good record when applied in practice. One of these theories is known as guided mastery. Developed by Bandura (1997), the theory states that novice learners and returning learners tend to make progress if tasks are broken down into readily mastered steps. Actually, Bandura (1997, p. 329) regards, 'mastery experience as the principal vehicle of personal change'. Insofar as self-doubting people are concerned, the taste of success is a disconfirming proof of their misgivings. The role of the social pedagogue in such circumstances is to create enabling conditions so that insecure people can perform well, "despite themselves".

Actually, enablement is a central pillar in social pedagogic work, and its long pedigree is found in some of the great foundational texts. Notable here, is the work of Natorp (1904), who thought that social pedagogy could offer the pedagogic wherewithal for individuals and groups (especially, groups) to recognise the infinite potential of socially responsible human wilfulness. Karl Mager, a famous predecessor of Natorp, held similar views. Mager believed that social pedagogy should play a major role in the nurturing of Bildung, understood here as the unfolding of the child's innate self-efficacy (cf. Mathiesen, 2008). Importantly, the unfolding process involves a growth in self-belief, that is to say, a sense of being in control and of being able to take control when circumstances demand so.

Drawing out an individual's perception of her agentic sway is a critical social pedagogic task, particularly when social pedagogues seek to enhance the confidence and poise of self-doubting people. A helpful strategy here is the use of 'performance mastery aids' (Bandura, 1997), which, when skilfully applied, can trigger perceived self-efficacy. By way of illustration, Bandura recommends the modelling of feared activities in order to demonstrate that the catastrophic beliefs that very anxious people hold do not actually happen. Returning to the example I gave above, a confident job-seeker might be asked to model this self-assured behaviour to the insecure job-seeker. Perhaps, for instance, the less confident applicant might observe the model preparing a CV. This offers the opportunity to see someone in a similar situation performing a task well. There is a cue here. The doubter is tacitly invited to imitate the other's behaviour by carrying out the same assignment. It is important to stress the importance of invitation here, because an offer, unlike an edict, respects individual identity and affinity.

KEY QUESTION
What is it about respect for individual agency in a learning situation, insofar as
this is feasible, that attracts social pedagogic attention?

The observation of proficient modelling can be a helpful practice in
social pedagogy. It is based on the theory of observational learning,
which posits that by watching skilful models, learners might be able to
transcend the limitations of their immediate circumstances (Bandura,
1997). Having extracted the main features (and when ready, the finer
details), the novice learner can, if so inclined, try them out. Outcomes
will of course vary. If things go well, the social pedagogue is there to
praise, and to do so with emotional enthusiasm. If things do not go well
first time, she is there to encourage and support. Repeated efforts will
surely lead to a successful episode, and the learner will have discovered
that perseverance pays off. One successful mastery experience can be
enough to enhance efficacy beliefs and improve later performance. This,
in turn, can help insecure people to grasp that they really can exert a level
of control over their lives. There are, though, circumstances in which
perceived self-efficacy is not enough to overcome adversity. The
condition of being poor and hungry in an uncaring environment is a
relevant example.

Such overwhelming obstacles are recognised in the cognitive theory of
stress, developed by the American psychologist, Richard S. Lazarus
[1922-2002] (Lazarus & Folkman, 1984). At the same time, this
important theory offers hope to people who tend to over-exaggerate
perceived problems. Lazarus (1993) has repeatedly found that those who
appraise stressful conditions as controllable by action are likely to adopt
problem-focused coping strategies. Furthermore, planned problem-
solving and positive re-appraisal is associated with emotional changes:
from negative to less negative or positive (Lazarus, 1993).

So reliable theory, when acted upon, offers the potential to produce
desirable outcomes. This is why contemporary social pedagogy needs a
robust theoretical foundation in order to help people to acknowledge and
act upon their capacity for successful change agency. Sometimes, on its
own and unapplied to practice, theory is just an idea about an idea. But
that is alright too. It is often necessary to think abstractly if a relevant
idea about practice is to hatch. Being too hasty in applying a theory is
unwise. Even so, when a good theory does surface, it is prudent to try it

out in the practical world, to test it. In social pedagogy, social programmes often arise from credible theories. Nevertheless, it would be rash to suggest that theory can solve every puzzle. Indeed, Popper (2007, p. xv) notes that philosophers face, 'something resembling a heap of ruins (though perhaps with treasure buried underneath).' Although those words were first published in 1934, by allusion, they still remind social scientists that social life is not neat and tidy.

At the same time, the caution lays down a challenge: in theory, there is an opportunity for better understanding. Unlike in Continental Europe, however, where social pedagogic theory has a relatively long history, social pedagogy in the UK is still getting to grips with relevant concepts. A reason for this is that the discipline is a recent arrival in the home country. This explains why there are so few published texts on social pedagogy in the English language. Actually, much of the foundational writing in the mid-19th and early 20th centuries was in German and remains so. The problem is especially grave with regard to social pedagogic theory. Frankly stated, some English theoretical texts are spare in detail and even whimsical.

What is theory?

Academics and practitioners often distinguish between theory and practice. In this chapter, the focus is on theory, but the two do intersect. The word "theory" has its origin in the Greek "Θεωρία" ("theoria"). In Ancient Greece, theory referred to a contemplative gaze. This is an obliging depiction because it underlines the worth of vigilant observation. Today, "theory" is regarded as the branch of a discipline that deals with its concepts and provisional explanation as distinguished from its practice.

KEY DEFINITION

Broadly speaking, theory has two main characteristics:

- It represents (through systematic concepts) the nature of the real world.

- It proposes explanations (usually as hypotheses) about things in the real world.

To consider *representation* first, social pedagogic concepts are only as good as they resemble reality. To the extent it is possible to take a social pedagogic concept (e.g. guided mastery) at face value, is a measure of the concept's power to reflect that reality accurately. One way of finding if it does, is to see if lots of people attach the same meaning to the concept. With regard to *explanation*, many social pedagogic ideas are initially formulated as hypotheses that may or may not work in practice. If these hypotheses are not falsified, they can provisionally be accepted as plausible. The longer a hypothesis stands its ground, the more credible it becomes. For example, the hypothesis that perceived self-efficacy (agentic belief in oneself) promotes coping skills is supported by solid evidence.

To cite one particular study, Jones (2006) notes that social cognition theory and the conception of self-efficacy underpin many self-management programmes for chronic disease. She adds that self-efficacy promoting interventions predict better levels of functioning and mental well-being. If UK policymakers are serious about introducing social pedagogy into the education of the child workforce, they will need to ensure that social pedagogic work has strong theoretical foundations. Put simply, theory must figure prominently in college and university courses, as well as in-service education and training.

Before going further, it is necessary to say something about epistemology – namely, how we justify that what we believe to be real (our theory) is actually real, and, in the case of social issues, why one kind of reality (e.g., social justice) is morally better than another. Social pedagogy uses evidence and value judgement here. Consider, for example, the problem of poverty in society. To be poor, means to have a significantly unequal share of the national cake. This is measurable, but a value judgement must be made regarding the cut-off point; namely, the income level below which a person is deemed to be poor. I could add other items, such as wealth, but I want to keep things simple for present purposes. Social pedagogy, being an emancipatory discipline, is forthright about poverty levels. In a socially just society, incomes should be shared much more equally. This is, at it were, the calculus of social justice, not of arithmetic.

Once that moral decision is settled, though, then statistics do come into play. Thus, in an enlightened society, the distance between the highest net income above the median and the lowest net income below the median should be short. For example, if the median net income in an imagined society is £2000 per month, highest earners might receive about £2400 per month and lowest earners might get about £1600.

In such a utopian society, it might be possible to claim that there is no poverty because nobody has too much, nobody has too little and everyone has enough money to enjoy a socially dignified life. The epistemology in that particular context can be stated as follows. Income is, by and large, shared by all (the mathematical proof) and this is fair (the value judgment). The evidential aspect is number; the judgmental part is ethical argumentation (see, for example, Rawls, 2003).

In defence of social pedagogic theory

During an address to the Annual Institute of the Society for Social Research at the University of Chicago in 1937, the legendary American sociologist, Talcott Parsons [1902-1979] (1938, p. 13), cited a statement that Max Weber [1864-1920] (a German founding father of sociology) was fond of: 'In order to understand Caesar it is not necessary to have been Caesar'. Being primarily a theorist at that time, Parsons wanted to persuade his audience that theory can help to illuminate empirical issues. His own voluminous theory was testimony to that argument, and later became an important touchstone for empirical research in sociology. Indeed, for Parsons (1968, p. 69), 'scientific theory … is justified only by its usefulness in understanding the facts of empirical experience.'

Theories are the result of serious pondering, and provide an understanding of a complex and often confusing world. They arise from empirical evidence, but not fully finished; so they need to be tested by empirical methods. Some theories are found to be dependable, others not so. This consideration is crucially important if people are to be able to avoid obstacles in life or to overcome them. Choosing the right theory is more likely to bring about the desired results. In that conceptual framework, rigorous social pedagogic theory serves as a reliable guide for equipping people with robust social and, to a lesser extent, cognitive skills. This is best achieved through the learning and habituating of efficacious thoughts and actions. Because social pedagogy is mainly concerned with solving social problems, social pedagogic practice mainly aims to help disadvantaged individuals and groups to gain more control over matters that adversely affect them.

The aim is to find and execute ways of securing desired consequences, such as social justice, and to prevent undesirable ones, such as poverty. There is something very Aristotelian about this. In his (350 B.C.E.)

renowned work, *Nichomachean Ethics*, the legendary Greek philosopher distinguished between intellectual and moral virtues. According to Aristotle, intellectual virtue included practical wisdom. Today, that is sometimes referred to as science, applied wisely. The resonance with social pedagogic practice derives from the virtue of enlisting the intellect in the pursuit of socially just projects. That knowledge makes it more likely that such projects will lead to intended benefits. As for moral virtue, Aristotle equated this with liberality and being good-tempered.

Through individual and collective learning, people can improve their life chances by changing, insofar as this is possible, unhelpful habits and unjust social systems. At the core of this endeavour, personal and collective efficacy has a major role to play. People must also take responsibility for each other. If that were to happen on a much larger scale, social pedagogues would be out of a job, and for the right reason. But it has not and they are not. So in the meantime, social pedagogic work is pledged to nurturing 'infinite benevolence toward the other' (Lévinas et al, p. 199, 2006), while simultaneously removing or ameliorating the suffering of those who have great hardship in life. This latter goal requires responsive intervention after the fact, such mediation being often referred to as "crisis social pedagogy". On its own, crisis social pedagogy does not change macro-structures, which means that it is not a vehicle of social change. However, it can help to ameliorate private problems.

KEY DEFINITION
Crisis social pedagogy is interventionist; the aim is to remove or ameliorate acute social problems after they have already arisen.

It is difficult, if not impossible, to work out the mathematical ratio between preventative and responsive practice in social pedagogy. The problem of calculation is even more elusive in the theoretical realm, which is harder to quantify. I think that in a (relatively speaking) socially just society, crisis social pedagogy will be in short supply for good reason: children who internalise kind values and a sense of purpose are more likely to become kind and confident adults. However, in societies where social disadvantage persists – basically, all in varying degrees – crisis social pedagogy is in big demand. For all that, attending to pressing individual needs should not halt the quest for social solidarity and social justice on the route to a better society.

KEY QUESTION

Give some concrete examples of real or imagined situations that need to be dealt with through crisis social pedagogy? Justify your reasoning.

Regardless of whether social pedagogy has a preventative or a responsive function (or, indeed, both), Bandura's (1997) concept of self-efficacy has theoretical and practical significance. Trusting in one's ability to manage life, brings its own reward. The important message here is that anyone can draw upon innate efficacy if they believe they can (cf. Lazarus & Folkman, 1984). The prize is a positive appraisal of the challenge ahead and, as a consequence, serious effort. This, in turn, will bring success sooner or later, itself usually a portent of even further accomplishments. As indicated, social pedagogues are enablers. They seek to enable socially disadvantaged people to overcome personal and structural challenges. With regard to the individual level, this involves understanding, in a non-judgemental way, how a person perceives her life.

This is essentially a cognitive matter and concerns the "head". If the person seeks help because he perceives daily routines to be overwhelming undertakings, the social pedagogue might apply ideas from cognitive psychology in order to assist. For example, a degree of "re-learning" in order to cultivate solution-focused thinking could be helpful. Then there is the "heart", which gently presents itself through emotional support and encouragement. Hearts feel and are guided by affect. In the social pedagogic relationship, both parties are obliged to adopt a "we" perspective from which each perceives the other as a subject. It follows from this that arriving at a well-founded consent is better served by an emotional atmosphere that is non-coercive and munificent (cf. Habermas, 2005).

The "hands" are essential too. They summon cognition and affect, particularly in creative work, which can stimulate self-starting contemplation and fervent imagination. In this setting, learners can initiate their own projects, self-express and figure out their "problems" (cf. Friesen & Sævi, 2010). This turns traditional pedagogic practices involving teacher-led activities on their head.

In the above head-heart-hands trilogy, social pedagogic work functions on three levels but in a holistic way. Notwithstanding, cognition, affect and practice will be weighted differently according to specific contexts. In that configuration, there is an assumption: people will enhance their capacity for learning and applying social skills if they know that the social pedagogue sincerely cares for them. What this means is that even the social pedagogic enabling of instrumental solutions is an act of love, a willing gift in the service of social justice.

The heart, of course, is a metaphor that denotes compassion and concern, especially for the less fortunate. In this vocabulary, there is no place for the oxymoron, "tough love". On the contrary, social pedagogic work, like social work (cf. Webb, 2007), is dedicated to the comfort of strangers. There are historical precedents. Natorp's (1904) foundational theory of social pedagogy envisaged a society based on community values. Indeed, for him, a human being only becomes *de facto* a part of humanity when attached to the wider community. For this reason, Natorp anticipated a close alliance between social pedagogic movements and the democratization of public life. When, as envisaged in Natorp's theory, the good intentions of individuals converge into the best interests of the many, social pedagogy is on a quest for solidarity. That involves the splicing of theory and ethics for the common good. I briefly referred to Natorp's pivotal role in the development of social pedagogic theory in Chapter 1. I will consider his work in more detail later in the present chapter.

With regard to social pedagogic theory in general, I have yet to see significant inroads in the UK. Yet in spite of British pragmatism, Moss and Petrie (2002) insist that theory is necessary when thinking about social pedagogic policy. A starting point here might be, 'what is our image of the child?' (Moss & Petrie, 2002, p. 22). The authors argue that a convincing reply must address several dimensions. The implication is that a plausible "adult theory" of the child needs to be multi-faceted. When they answer the rhetorical question that they pose, Moss and Petrie (2002, p. 23) apply a concept of the child as, 'rich in potential, strong, powerful, competent and, most of all, connected to adults and other children'. This is an optimistic viewpoint because it encourages social pedagogues to see promise in every child. A practical implication would be to find and act on the spark that ignites the child's innate capacities. The deserved accolade also positions children as agents who have self-enabling capacities.

Indeed, even in cases of serious threats to their own healthy development, children are often more resilient than assumed, and with encouraging results (Masten, 2001). Resilience derives from what Masten (2001, p. 235) refers to as:

'the everyday magic of ordinary, normative human resources in the minds, brains, and bodies of children, in their families and relationships, and in their communities. This has profound implications for promoting competence and human capital in individuals and society.... The conclusion that resilience emerges from ordinary processes offers a far more optimistic outlook for action than the idea that rare and extraordinary processes are involved.'

This is music to the ears of social pedagogues, who play a key role in helping socially disadvantaged children and adults to summon inner resilience in hard times. Ultimately, that comes down to assisting people to believe in their own capacity to get things done: properly supported, of course. The theorising behind that insight owes much to Positive Psychology, which emphasises the benefit of optimistic thinking as against the burden of dwelling on failure. This buoyant psychology poses a crucial question: "What capabilities does a person have in order to deal positively with life?" (cf. Snyder & Shane, 2002). Social pedagogy certainly counts efficacy beliefs among such capabilities, especially when these convictions are welded into collective purpose.

KEY QUESTION
Are social pedagogues justified in thinking that people really can perceive and mobilise innate capacities in order to change things for the better in life?

On that note, it is heartening to find inspiration in classic social pedagogic theory.

Foundational theory in social pedagogy

The origins of classic social pedagogic theory are found, as stated earlier, in Germany during the period from the mid-19th century to the early 20th century. Among the most significant pioneers, Paul Natorp (1854-1924) and Herman Nohl (1879-1960) are prominent. Interestingly, Nohl (cf. Hämäläinen, 2003) regarded social pedagogy as an educative process based on compassionate values, whose aim was to promote self-help and to do so in an instrumental rather than an expressive way. This emphasis on the nurturing of self-efficacy through a labour of love still remains at the heart of contemporary social pedagogy in Continental Europe.

Even though the discipline clearly has much to offer the Anglophone world (where social pedagogy is in the early stages of development), to the chagrin of translators, much of the early German writing contains convoluted grammar and long sentences. This was not uncommon in the dry, academic German of the time. Perhaps this explains why so little of the foundational literature on social pedagogy has been translated into English. Nonetheless, I have been fortunate to receive expert help from three German academics, one of them a Professor of Social Pedagogy. Their guidance has assisted me in translating an influential definition of social pedagogy that comes from the pen of Natorp himself (1904, p. 94):

KEY DEFINITION

'The social aspects of education, broadly understood, and the educational aspects of social life constitute this science' [social pedagogy]. My brackets.

Now that you have a working definition to hand, have a go at answering the following question.

KEY QUESTION

What is your understanding of Natorp's (1904) understanding of social pedagogy?

In a stroke of genius, Natorp (1904) has laid bare the essence of social pedagogic theory. He has identified the *social in the educational* and the *educational* in the *social*. To put it another way, education is a social process and social life is an educational process. This might sound obvious. However, the dichotomization of the "social" and the "educational" into distinct domains has strong roots in the UK, where social care and schooling have often been seen as separate functions. Yet for Natorp (1904, p. 94), education and social life were inseparable because, 'The concept of social pedagogy recognises that the education of the individual ... is socially conditioned'.

KEY TASK

Provide some concrete examples of life events in which social and pedagogic (i.e., educational) dimensions are inextricably linked. Explain your reasoning.

For all the luminosity in Natorp's (1904) words, his definition is a discovery, not a creation. The educational and the social have always been connected, but the association has often been overlooked. Yet even in strict Victorian schools, how teachers managed pupils in classrooms unveiled the social in the educational, and games like cricket and rugby divulged the educational in the social. Natorp (1904) envisaged education and socialisation as overlapping processes. Actually, he came very close to using these terms as synonyms. But if it is possible to make a distinction, then socialisation is a more expansive process than education. Even so, education, in a broad sense, is surely the main vehicle of socialisation. As a German, Natorp used the term "Bildung" when referring to education. This is significant because, in German, Bildung denotes, among other things, personal and social development, which are key areas of social pedagogic concern. Prange's (2004) notion of Bildung as an educational "extra" that nurtures grace-perfecting nature is interesting. At the same time, it is pertinent to note that the English word, "education" is also broad enough to denote the personal and social aspects of learning.

Natorp's (1904) magnum opus had a clear moral agenda, and the lengthy cover title of the book shows the hope he had for social pedagogy as a project. This is the title:

> Sozialpädagogik. Theorie der Willenserziehung auf der Grundlage der Gemeinschaft [Social Pedagogy: The Theory of Educating the Human Will into a Community Asset]

The project is thus to educate people to commit to making a contribution for the benefit of the community. Natorp is here calling for the planned socialisation/education of children and adults into values and norms that reflect and support solidarity. In his book, he also tacitly recognises the significance of incidental learning by invoking the idea of informal education in settings that are predominantly social (e.g. play). Based on expert opinion received from the German social pedagogue, Professor Heinz Sünker, it also seems likely that Natorp (1904) approved of Ferdinand Tönnies's (1855-1936) idealisation of community life (cf. Tönnies, 2009).

The two thinkers were friends and neo-Kantians of similar stripes. Tönnies, also German, is a "founding father" of sociology. The neo-Kantian leanings that he and Natorp shared are particularly significant. The German philosopher, Immanuel Kant (1724-1804), believed in an ethical community founded on mutual trust, where individual decisions would be based on actions to which everyone would consent. This perspective was to become firmly rooted in foundational social pedagogic theory in Germany, with Natorp as its champion. For his part, Tönnies (2009) published a landmark book in 1887, *Community and Civil Society*, in which he examined the differences and tensions between Gemeinschaft and Gesellschaft (Small Community and Large Society, respectively). In a pure Gemeinschaft – rarely found in real life but often approximated – 'there is a complete unity of human wills' (Tönnies, 2009, p. 22). This strong collective ethos is based on enduring kinship and neighbourhood bonds.

In Gesellschaft, on the other hand, wilfulness is deeply personal:

'... everyone is out for himself alone and living in a state of tension against everyone else' (Tönnies, 2009, p. 52).

Tönnies, (2009, p. 256) argues that, 'the big city, and *Gesellschaft* conditions in general, are the ruin and death of the people.' Although he regarded his book as an academic rather than a moral text, Tönnies sympathised with Gemeinschaft and was distrustful of Gesellschaft. There are clear parallels between his approving accounts of community life (some disparaging asides admitted) and Natorp's (1904) belief in communal solidarity. It is instructive to note that Natorp's (1904) social pedagogic goal of fashioning individual wills into a communal will resonates with what Bruner (1996, p. 45) insists is the:

'one "presenting problem" that is always with us in dealing with teaching and learning .... the issue of how human beings achieve a meeting of minds ...'

Interestingly, Titmuss (1997), who studied the ethics of blood donation, also had ideals that Natorp would surely have supported. In the UK, where donors give their blood for free, theirs is an act of altruism that, 'attempts to fuse the politics of welfare and the morality of individual wills' (Titmuss, 1997, p. 59).

Tönnies's (2009) Gemeinschaft model – undoubtedly idealised but still approximated in some social settings – envisages a life style based on cohesion. That value is also found in Bandura's (1997) conception of 'perceived collective efficacy'. This is efficacy on the march, fuelled by a group's or a community's belief that its members have the power to change social arrangements. Once set in motion, as Natorp (1904) understood, cooperative energy can recast individual wills into a unified social will. What is more, a strong belief in pulling together produces formidable results when put into practice. Consider, for example, Martin Luther King's famous "I have a dream ..." speech in 1963 from the steps of the Lincoln Memorial in Washington DC.

This glorious speech, the cornerstone of the largest civil rights demonstration ever in the US, united the common hopes of an audience of 250,000 people. The social momentum sparked by Dr King's stalwart conviction and illustrious oratory changed the course of history. In 1965, with the support of the civil rights movement and its friends, President Johnson had driven through Congress and signed into law the Civil Rights and Voting Rights Acts. The legislation confirmed that the federal government would, at long last, support ethnic integration. These Acts were the result of perceived collective efficacy on a momentous scale. Moreover, the legislation shows that united action by ordinary people can fell unethical political systems. On a more modest level, social pedagogues can galvanise community engagement by supporting neighbourhood initiatives, such as creating an accessible built environment for wheelchair users.

Community knowledge – the people's knowledge – often stands in stark contrast to academic knowledge – the expert's knowledge. Bernstein's (2000) notion of 'vertical discourse' is relevant here. It represents an institutional or official pedagogy couched in the language of a learned elite. The upshot is, well, a "vertical", strongly codified conversation (in its oral form) in which specialists are at the top, and ordinary folk are in the foothills. A meeting between a no-nonsense doctor and a compliant patient comes to mind. By contrast, a bi-lateral form of communication between the doctor and the patient would signify a horizontal, social pedagogic approach.

Returning to Natorp (1904, p. VI), his aim, in his own words, was, 'to address a crucial and a contemporary question: the relationship between education and community'. More specifically, he placed social pedagogy in the service of community socialisation and brought democracy into the public sphere. There are parallels with the conviction of the towering French sociologist, Emile Durkheim (1858-1917) (1980, p. 79), 'that education is an eminently social thing in its origins as in its functions ...' Like Durkheim, Natorp also thought that individuals become social human beings through socialisation into the bigger collective (cf. Mathiesen, 1999).

Preparation for social life, very much a pedagogic task, is at the centre of Natorp's (1904) social pedagogy. This function is still regarded as pivotal in social pedagogic practice. Petrie et al (2006, p. 23) exemplify the point when they highlight a 'pedagogy of relationships' in the social spaces that social pedagogues and children often share. These spaces have a vital role in getting children ready for associative life in society. Keeping with this theme, it should be noted that social pedagogues seek to enlarge what Lewin (2000, p. 16), calls a 'space of free movement'. This could involve, for example, letting children choose their favourite activities in after-school clubs. At the same time, the child's safety must be at the forefront of social pedagogic practice. That is why Lewin's (2000, p. 19) other idea of an intermediate social space permitting 'degrees of freedom' is important. In this space, some activities might be allowed while others could be entirely prohibited.

KEY TASK

Describe a setting where children could occupy what Lewin (2000, p. 16) refers to as a 'space of free movement'.

At the other end of the continuum, are complete limitations on freedom. Charles Dickens's *Oliver Twist* exemplifies the condition. The young Oliver is raised in a Victorian orphanage run by the monstrous Mrs Mann and Mr Bumble, whose idea of child upbringing is total control. For this reason, social pedagogy can never stand for a model of socialisation based on the uncritical reproduction of prevailing customs. If such were so, change agency would be impossible because some children would be protégés of dictatorial significant others. Social pedagogy rejects totalitarian forms of socialisation because this defeats the very purpose of helping people to change life for the better, and in dialogue with them. Put another way, social pedagogues seek the reconstruction of society through the reconstruction of the child (see Popkewitz, no date). The decisive role that the younger generation play in social change is familiar. It is known as history in the making.

Does social pedagogic theory promote specific norms?

The term, "norms", refers to conduct based on socially approved values; as for the question, the reply is a resounding, "Yes". Social pedagogy has always stood for socially approved values, some of them noble, others shameful. In general though, social pedagogy has supported social solidarity, which stands in stark contrast to social division. Social solidarity, to borrow from Rawls (2003) [see Chapter 4], prizes more rather than less freedom and a greater rather than a smaller share of income and wealth. From these moral precepts (or values), arise normative practices, namely, respecting others' liberty and striving for an egalitarian society.

The normative goal of social pedagogy is thus to create a society where tolerance looms large and one in which social justice predominates, here understood as a fair society where nobody is a "have-not".

KEY QUESTION(S)

Does or could such a society exist, or is the notion of a tolerant, socially just society just a pipe-dream? If you think that such idealised perfection is unachievable, is it realistic to believe that human beings can get close to the target?

Consider in that light Natorp's (1904) social pedagogy. He had a conception of a discipline that would nurture solidarity based on mutual respect and community spirit. It is apposite to add that Natorp was a self-confessed socialist and that socialism, as a political creed, endorses social solidarity. So, without doubt, social pedagogic theory is candidly normative, often with left-wing but also democratic leanings. For Natorp (1904), the challenge for social pedagogy was to derail the Gessellschaft locomotive of societal fragmentation, which led to the pursuit of self-interest and neglect of the common good. The normative means for avoiding a society full of selfish people was therefore civic engagement in the service of Gemeinschaft values (cf. Smith, 2009).

Natorp's (1904) and Tönnies's (2009) philosophies are woven from the same cloth. Both men were committed to the democratisation of public life, which involves a shift of emphasis from schooled knowledge to local knowledge (cf. Bernstein, 1999). The former has its origins in the aloof intellect of the head (the bodily part, not the head teacher!), the latter in the temperate impulses of the heart (cf. Tönnies's, 2009). And where is social pedagogy in this dichotomy? It lies along a continuum, but is weighted towards the heart.

Social pedagogy is not just a "Large Society Mover"; it also supports the poor and oppressed on a face-to-face level. On this plane, it proposes individual solutions, such as lifting the spirits of a dejected human being, as well as celebrating, enlisting and supporting the person's potential to fashion a better future. Enablement is the key tool here because it can turn helplessness into taking charge. Not only does social pedagogic theory seek to promote, on the service user's premise, helpful social functioning, it also supports parity in conversations with oppressed individuals. This entails shortening the distance between the conversationalists so that both feel they have a right to be heard. For example, when counselling an adolescent in a residential home on post-16 study options, the social pedagogue avoids imposing her views on the young person. She dispenses advice and respectfully listens to his proposals. She also affirms the young person's right to exercise control over his own life. Both persons have different roles, but as human beings they are equals.

Habermas's (2005) work is especially relevant with regard to democratic dialogue. In his study of how people enter dialogues with each other, Habermas endorses the unforced force of the better argument. His theory, which goes by the complex name of 'communicative action', boils down to a compelling proposition: the correct basis for claiming that a proposition is true, is that it was arrived at through convincing argumentation, and that all discussants see eye to eye on the conclusion. In a social pedagogic sense, such mediation involves the head and the heart, namely, sound logic and right conviction. If logic alone could turn the heart towards righteous action, then social pedagogy would have little interest in spontaneous feeling. But such is not the case. Logic and feeling can, however, support each other in the cause of natural justice. The mathematical logic for slicing a cake into five equal pieces for five people and the moral feeling that sharing is fair, illustrates this point.

There is, though, a warning. Feeling is often intuitive. This is wonderful when intuited action leads to dignified outcomes, but not when a misguided hunch or an angry outburst is harmful.

A contemporary theory of social pedagogy

Founding Fathers such as Natorp (2004) developed original theories of social pedagogy. But their pioneering ideas were written more than a century ago. There is nothing wrong with that, but like any social science, social pedagogy is a developing discipline. This is why it is necessary to cultivate new concepts and fresh ideas. In this section, I seek in a modest way to engage that brief. It is not my intention, however, to relegate foundational theory to the annals of history. Instead, I seek to combine critical foundational positions with contemporary points of view, the latter mainly drawn from social psychology and pedagogy.

One of the most important contemporary thinkers in that context is Bandura. The title of his best known book, *Self-Efficacy* (1997), indicates his field of study, and I have earlier referred to this important work. But to recapitulate, self-efficacy refers to a person's capability to exercise influence over her own life. This refers, in particular, to the capacity of making positive changes in life. For example, a person might overcome a fear of going to cafés by determinedly visiting them until the anxiety drifts away, which it probably will do. The outcome is a change in thinking and acting that brings benefits, such as enhanced confidence and an enriched social life.

In their book, *Education for Social Justice*, Chapman and West-Burnham (2010) turn their attention to social pedagogy. They correctly note that the discipline combines the work and values of social workers and teachers, adding that social pedagogy addresses, 'the need, as appropriate, for restorative and compensatory intervention to build personal capacity.' (p. 152). This argument strikes a chord with Bandura (1997), who believes that psychologists have a crucial role in developing perceived self-efficacy. It is important here to note the adjective, "perceived". This denotes that self-efficacy (or personal capacity) is a starting point. It has to be believed in and with conviction; otherwise, there is the danger that it will remain dormant.

Bandura (1997, p. 3), as made clear, uses the term 'perceived self-efficacy' to denote a person's belief in her personal capability to produce desired results. Moreover, he (1997, p. 3) believes that this sense of self-management is, 'the key factor of human agency'. Social pedagogues agree. The onus is on discarding erroneous yet felt feelings of incapacity, which hamper realistic potential. The pedagogic dimension of social pedagogy has much to offer here. Consider again, the person with a fear of visiting cafés. Through dialogue with a social pedagogue, both might agree that employing the services of a personal assistant would help her to make bold forays into the "dreaded locations". After a degree of habituation, she might then feel confident to go it alone, thereby increasing opportunities for social networking in public places. The next step would be to consolidate early victories by making them a routine part of an adjusted habitus. This takes practice. But the reward is a reliable social script and confidence in it (perceived self-efficacy) for future reference.

Bandura's (1997) theory also extends the analysis of self-efficacy to the added impetus of collective efficacy. This recalls Natorp's (1904) argument that the human will thrives within the bigger tapestry of community. People need to get along together and support each other to make a better life for themselves. In the contemporary language of Bandura (1997, p.402), the goal is, 'to forge a sturdy sense of group efficacy from a collection of individuals and to sustain it in the face of setbacks and defeats'. This is a tough challenge, but when applied effectively, it fosters a collective perception of efficacy and common purpose, the perfect Gemeinschaft, in fact.

Bandura (1997) illustrates the point in the context of neighbourhood improvement. He identifies the key role here of the dedicated community organiser, who acts as a catalyst by serving as the 'enabler rather than the implementer of action plans. The initial task is to search out and develop local leaders who can unite the community for common cause' (Bandura, 1997, p. 501). The enabler role is paramount in social pedagogy. Enablers set up optimal conditions for efficacy building and then step back a little. They are experts at scaffolding and guided mastery and equally good at removing ramparts when self- and collective efficacy beliefs take over and finish the job.

Guided mastery and scaffolding come from the same stable. Indeed, they are almost synonyms. But there is a subtle difference. Scaffolding is a transitory form of support (e.g. a driving simulator adapted for a disabled learner) and is steadily removed as progress is observed. Guided mastery, on the other hand, refers to a pedagogue's judgment about when to take away a bit of scaffolding, or when not to do so. Essentially, the pedagogue needs to consider the following question:

Can the learner consistently perform a fully scaffolded task well?

If the answer is yes, the next step is to stimulate more self-reliant learning by removing some of the props. If the answer is no, it is best to leave things as they are until the learner can perform the task in a shielded setting.

Once the dismantling starts, pieces are moved one at a time. The ultimate pedagogic aim (both cognitive and social), which is reached through consensual dialogue, is to promote optimal and independent mastery in a scaffold-free setting. It is relevant to point out that everyone, not just those going through hard times, requires a degree of scaffolding and guided mastery when they undertake new tasks. This applies, for example, to airline pilots, nurses, carpenters and social workers, to name but a few. Any learner who does not receive pedagogic support along the way, will find it hard to develop self-regulatory skills. The social pedagogic effort that goes into enabling perceived self-efficacy among people who are used to believing that things are beyond their control is formidable. It represents a decisive strategy for combating apathy and defeatism and promoting conviction and courage among individuals who have perhaps given up.

Groups also gain from scaffolding and guided mastery. Interdependence in the execution of challenging tasks is important but insufficient on its own. When, however, social pedagogic backing is to hand, joint endeavour gets a boost. Once the group gains a cognitive and social footing, its members can then fight for *their own* agenda. The resounding success stories of groups such as the Philadelphia-based Disabilities Rights Advocacy Group Inc. are testimony to this. This particular group has been a major lobbying force for building curb cuts along city pavements and for making ATMs accessible. Such actions have set in motion national trends. Illustrative of this, user-friendly ATMS now exist across the US. This is social pedagogy on the march.

KEY TASK

Consider and suggest what perceived collective efficacy might add to perceived self-efficacy. Illustrate your proposal(s).

The American polemicist, Michael Moore, highlighted the unstoppable force of "people power" in his eighth documentary film, *Capitalism: A Love Story* (2009). In the film, Moore maintains a resolute belief in the potential of community power to fix what politicians and bankers have broken. Consider, for example, the Michigan sheriff who refused to evict people from their foreclosed homes. Think about the Chicago factory workers who lost their jobs because of the recent global recession. In refusing to be fired empty-handed, they staged a sit-down protest and got the money entitlements that were owed to them. The "moral of the story" is that perceived collective efficacy helps people to solve the social problems that they face together.

Given that many life challenges are common problems and therefore require collective effort, this is not surprising. Nor is the fact that individuals on their own are often unable to exercise influence over major aspects of their lives. Through perceived collective efficacy, members of a community can come together as a united force based on their legitimate self-interests. This harkens back again to Natorp's (1904) fundamental argument that individual wilfulness must be pooled into collective effort. Unity can be further bolstered if members of a community unequivocally join around shared concerns. This could involve, for example, the lobbying of local politicians for better housing and for flexible forms of employment.

The wonderful thing about perceived collective efficacy in Gemeinschaft settings is that the theory actually works. Exemplifying this point, Bandura (1997) refers to the resounding success of a community leader in Texas who oversees a growing network of 150 community organisers and their delegates. The goal is to find collective solutions to obdurate educational problems. Organisers brief politicians on action plans for school reform and convene big, state-wide conventions. These collective actions gain political notice and bolster community influence. Once political goodwill is achieved, people are in a stronger position to exercise influence over political decision-making. But they must step carefully, seeking all the while after responsive leaders in the political elite. The aim is not to make (laudable though that is) but to influence policy, exploiting at every turn the small freedoms that democratic government makes available to local interest groups.

For example, community lobbying in support of better pay for migrant workers could begin by identifying a few political "heavy hitters" who work with immigration issues. A promising start might be to find senior politicians who have migrant roots. After that, their backing would be sought. Without going into further practical detail (that comes in the next chapter), there is a theoretical point to consider. Social systems, be they political, economic or otherwise, are structured but not completely so. There is unfinished business ripe for agentic action. There is also a proviso: aspiring change agents need to believe that they can effect a measure of transformation and need to persevere in the face of resistance.

Acting on efficacy beliefs will, sooner or later, self-fulfil, thereby attesting to Marx's famous axiom that people can make history even when circumstances are not of their own choosing.

Up to this point, I have identified a number of key theoretical principles in social pedagogy. So now, compared to the somewhat sparse offering in the preceding chapter, it is time to propose a fuller definition of the discipline.

Social pedagogy: a definition for today

Any definition of social pedagogy must contain two dimensions: the social and the pedagogic (or educational). Both elements are intertwined, but there are certain distinct features. Essentially, the social sphere is much bigger and more encompassing than the educational domain, even though the latter encroaches upon the former. But bond the two dimensions, and social pedagogy is the upshot. The weighting of each constituent part, the social and the pedagogic, will vary, a point made already. At times, social pedagogic interactions are more social than pedagogic and, at other times, more pedagogic than social. For example, small talk around a pot of coffee without pedagogic advice being dispensed is strongly social in nature. On the other hand, instructing a person on how to complete a social security form is more pedagogic than social.

In some contexts, the effects of the two parts are more or less equal, as happens, for example, in interactions that include learning based on modelling the social behaviour of others. This might occur when a child watches her dad politely order a cup of tea. The child, in turn, asks for a milkshake "please". Here is a case of successful replication, namely, imitative learning based on modelling another's behaviour. It is also important to recognise that subject learning involves a social relationship between the teacher and the student. Because, however, the parties are usually preoccupied with factual knowledge, that relational dimension is obscured; but it is still there. In fact, Natorp (1904, p. 94) claims that education is saturated with social aspects:

'The concept of social pedagogy inherently accepts that the education of the individual is social in all respects.'

In addition, education develops the faculty of societal critique, once again, showing its social origin. Some thinkers, notably Plato, believe that moral education not only produces a knowledge of the good, but also a propensity to do what is good. That said, there is no absolute guarantee that an educated person will behave well. For, as noted in Chapter 1, social pedagogues can act for good or ill. The dance between the "social" and the "educational" in social pedagogy, with each linked to the other, permits complex moves. This is helpful because social pedagogues seek specific solutions to specific problems rather than working from a pre-defined script. The focus is on the service user's unique needs.

Despite its educational pedigree, social pedagogy is hard to find in British schools. Indeed, it is often consigned to the elusive realm of the hidden curriculum. This out of sight "syllabus" comprises tacit expectations of how students should behave at school. It is written on the walls, so to speak. That makes it difficult for teachers to provide an education that explicitly promotes both cognitive and social learning. The cognitive part relies on subject teaching, the social part on a mix of implied norms and the vagaries of pastoral styles. But when the two pedagogies do embrace, the circle is completed. The end result is an education in the fullest sense.

Nevertheless, it is still right to distinguish broadly between a cognitive pedagogy that teaches facts and figures and a social pedagogy that instils social values and norms. There is a proviso, however. Even "facts and figures" teaching operates within a context. Do teachers expect to be addressed formally?, for example. Can pupils "butt in" if a Eureka moment occurs or must they put up their hands? Is group-work a normal part of the lesson? These are pressing questions, and they bring me back to the nature of social pedagogy as a discipline. I think that Natorp's (1904) conception of social pedagogy as a social science that investigates the social in the pedagogic and the pedagogic in the social is brilliantly insightful; so much so, that his foundational idea needs refining rather than replacing.

With that goal in mind and by piecing together some of Natorp's (1904) key ideas as well as relevant concepts from Bandura (1997) and a few thoughts of my own (Stephens, 2009), I propose below a tentative, even an hypothetical, definition of social pedagogy for today:

> **KEY DEFINITION**
>
> Social pedagogy is the social scientific study of planned and impromptu socialisation via the social learning and the emotional internalisation of values and norms.
>
> Typically, in planned socialisation, social pedagogues seek to enable perceived self- and group efficacy so that people can change their lives and society for the better. In most cases, planning and execution are decided through respectful dialogue involving the social pedagogue and the individual or the group. The aim is to reach agreement on a workable course of action.
>
> There is a crucial rejoinder. Individuals and groups are at liberty to plan their *own* socialisation to varying degrees by choosing how to live their *own* lives. At that juncture, the social pedagogue's role is to step back.

Defining a subject is invariably controversial. Academics and practitioners rarely reach agreement on the details. But they can usually be of the same mind on the main points. I think it might be helpful to see my take on social pedagogy as a conceptual hypothesis. That way, the definition can be adjusted, polished or even replaced by a better one. This flexibility makes it possible to develop compelling "I think" propositions rather than last-word "I know" statements. Popper's (2007) work is relevant here. He argues that propositions framed as hypotheses can only hold sway until a better argument prevails. True, his concern is with empirical hypotheses like, for example, "For every action force, there is an equal and opposite reaction force." However, the same principle applies to conceptual hypotheses, such as tentative definitions. When stated as hypotheses, Newton's Third 'Law' above or the definition of a subject, such as social pedagogy, are both open to scrutiny.

Even though the way I define social pedagogy must be seen as provisional, it serves a function. It makes my position clear to you, the reader. Moreover, you will, I hope, see its relevance in the next chapter, which pays particular attention to how social pedagogues are able to mobilise efficacy beliefs.

Heart and head

The reader will have noted the term, 'emotional internalisation', in my definition of social pedagogy. The idea that sociability can simply be learnt sits uneasily. Becoming social, necessarily involves *felt* norms and values, not simply rationally learnt rote knowledge. People feel rather than learn that something is right and something else is wrong. The "heart" rather than the "head" is at the helm here. Durkheim (1994) broached the issue of human morals when he proposed that moral judgements are found fully formed within us, even though we have not usually remembered elaborating them in a methodical way. He (1994, p. 192) added:

> 'This is why we so often imagine our moral conscience as a sort of voice which makes itself heard within us without our knowing as a rule what this voice is or whence its authority derives.'

But it comes from somewhere and it is internalised. The process starts in early life when the infant interacts with the human environment in which she develops. The more the infant (and later, the child) expands her social boundaries, first interacting with parents and siblings, then with other relatives and same-age peers, the more she exposes herself to different models of thinking and behaving. Selective imitation, an important part of the learning process, has a decisive role here. Thus, for example, seeing and trying out things that appeal to the child will probably play a significant part in internalisation. This is more likely to occur if the internalised behaviour attracts praise from respected significant others, such as parents. Moreover, what is internalised and repeated becomes habituated over time.

There are other ways – some of them more formalised, as in schooling – of internalising a social habitus. This raises the problematic question of social pedagogic ethics. If, for example the author embeds a very explicit judgment about the good society into a theory of social pedagogy, then the matter is "settled". The author's value then trumps other values, so to speak. A better alternative is to present a social scientific definition of the discipline and then to append this with Weber's (1949, p. 60) argument that, 'An *attitude of moral indifference* has no connection with *scientific* "objectivity"'. Afterwards, it is surely fitting to states one's own values honestly and openly.

Once this position is admitted, practice that is based on social pedagogic theory can serve a variety of ethical projects, wherever that may lead. Ethical ardour is often strong in the educational field. For example, in his struggle against illiteracy among American adults, Kozol (1986, p. xvii) states that his, 'feelings on this subject are too strong to be contained within an understated work'. He should be applauded for his passion and candour.

Concluding remarks

I believe in a social pedagogy that enlists the rationality of the head and the passion of the heart. The goal of this joint venture is to support the aspirations of those who are socially disadvantaged, as well as to help people in the vicinity of the danger zone. A critical question here is, who decides what these aspirations should be? Should the social pedagogue impose her values on the service user, or should the service user be free to choose his own future? There is a fine balance. Ultimately, the solution is to be found in an honest and courteous conversation of the kind that reaches a viable conclusion which both parties can agree upon. Once this is decided, enablement is reached.

In the next chapter, I shall examine social pedagogic practice, mindful of the fact that social pedagogic theory is a starting point that must bring practical benefits to individuals and society.

Chapter 3
Social pedagogic practice

'Well done is better than well said' (attributed to Benjamin Franklin)

Introduction

In the last chapter, I examined the text of social pedagogy, its theory. In this chapter, I investigate the deeds of social pedagogy, its practice. The word practice comes from the Greek praktiki (πρακτική), which means fit for action. The implication is that once theoretical understanding is in place (itself based on the rigorous study of the real world), then it is time to find out if the theory works in practice. Social pedagogic practice should be based, as far as possible, on fact-based evidence. Rigorous theory, sound research, dependable professional and service user knowledge all play a role here. Intelligent hunches also arise, but should be regarded as tentative until verified. Yet while an objective yardstick is essential for measuring the effects of social pedagogic interventions, how social pedagogy is practised must be based on clear values. An important question in that regard is, What kind of society do social pedagogues want to help create?

In Continental Europe, professional social pedagogues often work in social, health and educational services. In Norway, for example, their brief typically involves helping socially disadvantaged service users: the poor; the long-term unemployed; the chronically sick; victims of bullying, substance users; prisoners; and other vulnerable groups. In many cases, the presenting problems call for social pedagogic interventions that can be categorised as crisis work. How social pedagogues respond is a measure of their (and/or their organisation's) moral integrity. There is a power imbalance, weighted in favour of service professionals, but there is usually room for manoeuvre. This latitude, if acted upon justly, closes the distance between "experts" and "clients", thereby democratising the social pedagogic relationship.

This democratic turn invites the service user to contribute to the former question, so that it may be re-formulated as follows:

What kind of society do social pedagogues and those whom they serve wish to be a part of? This specific inquiry raises issues regarding value judgments and scientific veracity, and whether the two are compatible. The value dimension constitutes an ideological aspiration, namely, a belief in a society where individuals are able to participate in structural decisions that concurrently enhance their agency and well-being, as well as societal development (cf. Herrmann & van der Maesen, 2008). The scientific aspect addresses viability. Is this project doable and do value-judgments compromise objectivity?

Weber (1949, p. 60) enters the fray with characteristic aplomb: 'An *attitude of moral indifference* has no connection with *scientific* "objectivity".' He is right, of course. In fact, objectivity is the harbinger of effective and ethical social pedagogic practice. It gives clarity to social pedagogic problems and helps social pedagogues to make evidence-based decisions, thereby – crucial this – serving the human rights of the socially disadvantaged well. The point here is that, from a social pedagogic perspective, human suffering is not just a social problem but also a moral issue for society. Moreover, it is not a problem of "personal failure" (cf. Herrmann & van der Maesen, 2008).

Continuing the discussion on objective facts and moral decisions, Weber (1949, p. 51) helpfully distinguishes, 'between "existential knowledge", i.e., knowledge of what "is", and "normative knowledge", i.e., knowledge of what "should be". ' For example, 12 per cent of the adult population in Norway lived below the EU poverty line in 2008 (Normann, 2011). This is an objective fact. However, what to do about poverty is a value-judgment, even though any interventions should, of course, be scientifically unassailable. Because social pedagogues in Norway, where I work, undergo a professional education that explicitly promotes a concern for social justice (Stephens, 2011b), it is to be expected (or at least hoped) that they will attend to the needs of those most at risk in society, particularly the poor and oppressed. In normative terms, this means educating the service user to a better understanding of why her aspirations are not being met, as well as helping and supporting her to make advantageous changes in her life.

KEY QUESTION

How is it possible in social pedagogic practice to juxtapose, successfully, objective social science and subjective values? Use concrete or imagined examples to elucidate your argument.

There is also the macro-situation to consider. Social pedagogues who practise their profession compassionately, understand that their mandate is not just to help people in need but also concurrently to challenge what Mills (1973, p. 343) terms the 'higher immorality' that infiltrates 'the corporate worlds of business, war-making and politics'.

Decisions taken within these powerful circles frequently lead to a catalogue of injustices. Pushing through legislative remedies for social injustice requires either political muscle or access to and influence over it. Moreover, given the huge scale of wrongdoing in social policy circles, not to mention downright indifference to the plight of the poor, the social pedagogic task is a momentous one.

In the US, for example, lack of health insurance results in about 18,000 unnecessary deaths each year. This shocking statistic could be eliminated if politicians implemented a national health service based on clinical need rather than ability to pay. Not only do the 'men of affairs' (cf. Mills, 1973) defend the "ability to pay" system, they also enact legislation that makes it nigh impossible for health professionals to act on their conscience, namely, to be their Brother's Keeper, however poor she or he is.

Practice with a conscience

I am reminded of Bauman's (2009, p. 250) famous words: 'If in doubt – consult your conscience'. How hard this is to do when a social pedagogue's effort to act honourably is thwarted by a legislature that upholds an immoral society. In the stand-off, steps to alleviate immediate suffering – homelessness, poverty, unemployment and so on – must be the first priority. This often involves pedagogic efforts to change aspects of human behaviour – for example, resignation – so that socially disadvantaged people can escape from or alleviate some of the problems they face. At the same time, social pedagogues recognise that the root causes of most social problems lie within the structural failings of society.

The moral quandary for the practising social pedagogue then is what to do on the individual level here and now while constantly advocating on behalf of oppressed people to the powers that be. As for academic social pedagogues, they have a scientific and a moral responsibility to dispense policy advice that counsels against accounts of social problems that overestimate the effect of individual failings and underestimate the effects of institutional shortcomings. Speaking for myself, an academic social pedagogue, I avoid spending too much time in an ivory tower. As stated earlier, I also support and practise "street pedagogy".

This is social pedagogic work at close quarters and it involves not only practical support and "social tutoring", but also lobbying. I recently pulled a media stunt by sleeping one night on a railway bench previously occupied by a poor and sick Romanian migrant who had slept on it for three months during a fierce Norwegian winter. The aim was to increase public awareness about remedies that could prevent this from happening again. In addition, I sought to move some political consciences in local and national government. This undemanding, well-planned discomfort could have gone awfully wrong because there is little kindness for poor migrants in Norway. Fortunately though, the event drew a lot of public sympathy, always of use when rallying collective support. Shortly afterwards, Landsorganisasjonen i Norge (the Norwegian equivalent of the Trade Union Congress) invited me to speak on Labour Day (May 1, 2012) on an issue of my choice. I chose immigration policy.

In my 4-minute presentation, I appealed to the government to abandon so-called transitional rules that apply to migrant job-seekers from Bulgaria and Romania. These rules make it very difficult for persons from those countries to obtain the necessary paperwork for entry into the legal labour market. This is an example of structural oppression. On its own, of course, my voice has little impact on social policy. However, speaking from the podium of the most powerful labour organisation in the country might change that. I hope so anyway. Whether this is me in the role of professional actor (not in the Broadway sense!), is open to discussion. But I do believe that professors of social pedagogy should work in solidarity with the oppressed. They can do so, for example, by lobbying politicians and practising street pedagogy. Teaching and theorising then become part of the agenda, and do not crowd out moral purpose. Bourdieu is an inspirational role model here because his sociology of conviction was not just found in lecture halls, but also in Parisian slums.

Of particular relevance, street pedagogy, both face-to-face with the poor and as a civil advocate for them, has made me aware of how important it is to provide by-proxy support on their behalf. This is not to suggest that perceived efficacy is less important. On the contrary, it is the most important vehicle of social change. Yet how can oppressed people be expected to control institutional mechanisms that imprison them within "la grande misère" of structural injustice? They cannot. This is why social pedagogic work must confront the problem upon which matters of great and urgent importance hang: the social injustice of gaping inequality. That entails, based on the legacy of Natorp (1904), and many before and after him, a dedication to the common good. For therein lies the core of social justice: civic virtue (cf. Sandel, 2010).

There is, of course, no guarantee that social pedagogy will place itself in the service of this noble cause. I have earlier referred to social pedagogic practice in the furtherance of malign policy, not least during the era of the Third German Reich, where 'the pedagogization of all areas of life' promoted an ideology of "racial hygiene" (Sünker & Otto, 1997, p. vii). Even today, there are surely many examples of sociology and social pedagogy being put to misuse, as for example, in forced (but ineffective) efforts to re-socialise young offenders by sending them to brutalising boot camps. But in this book, unless specifically stated, my focus is on social pedagogy with a conscience, that is to say, a discipline committed to the cause of universal well-being. At its best, this entails changing unjust ways and replacing them with social justice, both individually and collectively. That is a hard task. But we have to try.

In the striving, the work of the social pedagogue must begin with children and continue into adulthood through the life course. For in children is found:

> 'Humanity at its best – undistorted, untruncated, untrimmed and unmaimed, whole in its childish inchoateness and nascence, full of as-yet-unbetrayed promise and as-yet-uncompromised potential' (Bauman, 2003, pp. 82-83)

Children's' lives represent the closest it is to epitomise Rawls's (2003) [see Chapter 4] uncorrupted original position, where fairness is theorised and idealised as a primordial ethic. In practice terms, the aim of the social pedagogue in this imagined setting would be (and can be in the real world also) to protect, 'the potential carriers of humanity' from a social system that is 'more adept at clipping wings than prompting the would-be flyers to spread them' (Bauman, 2003, p. 83). The task involves preventative and responsive work, respectively:

- preserving a child's inherent humanity by nurturing virtue

- intervening to rescue this humanity when the child goes astray by bringing her back to a universal moral reference point.

By way of practical illustration, this dual approach can:

- reinforce early-onset, virtuous behaviour, such as sharing a toy with another child

while at the same time

- help and support a child to comfort a victim of bullying instead of egging the bully on

The first example is preventative in the sense that the reinforcement of kindness averts selfishness. The second example is responsive because comforting a victim occurs after the fact.

KEY TASK

Describe two kinds of social pedagogic practice: one that is preventative, the other responsive. These can be real or imagined. Give reasons for your examples.

Prevention is better than cure

Preventative social pedagogic work with children, whether in family, pre-school, school, health or other settings, mainly focuses on interventions whose aim is to get all children off to a good start in life. Thus, for example, universal paediatric healthcare providing developmental monitoring and home visiting, and increasing parents' knowledge about how to enhance their children's well-being are all designed to head off potential risks (cf. Dworkin, 2003). Similarly, the provision of universal pre-school care and education promotes all-round positive child development, including cognitive achievement, sociability and concentration (Sylva et al, 2004).

If only such pre-emptive resources were available to all children, early risk factors would be stopped in their tracks. In particular, children who are raised by loving caregivers are off to a good start. What these caregivers do is to:

- establish stable bonds

- provide emotional refuge

- set applicable boundaries

- model civilised values and norms

- enable opportunities for appropriate mastery experiences

- support continuing opportunities for self-development

(cf. Bandura, 1997)

The above list could certainly be augmented, but whatever it adds up to, it not an inventory that guarantees a problem-free life. Nor does it replace the role of responsive (or crisis) social pedagogy. An auspicious opening bodes well, but does not mean that problems may (and probably will) arise that will require intervention. Notwithstanding, the odds for good life chances are generally favourable if the factors referred to above are in place. But what then about children who grow up in difficult conditions?

These might include:

- Poverty

- Parental mental illness

- Parental substance abuse

- Child abuse and neglect

- Teenage motherhood

- Serious trauma (e.g. war)

(cf. Werner, 2003).

Once again, this inventory is far from exhaustive. At the same time, it should not be viewed as an inevitable harbinger of awful things to come. Even so, the odds of unfavourable developmental outcomes are high, especially when multiple risks are present. In particular, poverty puts children at increased exposure to a multitude of problems from the moment of conception. Moreover, material hardship ushers in a host of other risk factors, including: in vitro exposure to toxic substances,

67

difficult birth outcomes, malnutrition, post-neonatal mortality, inattentive parental care, asthma and elevated blood lead levels (Halpern, 2003).

Most poor families do what they can for their children under exceedingly difficult circumstances. Yet the many damaging correlates of poverty can undermine even the most heroic efforts. For example, a significant number of young socially disadvantaged parents find it hard to muster the minimal personal, social and economic resources that are needed to meet their children's developmental needs (cf. Halpern, 2003). Some of these parents have personal histories punctuated with major problems, including disruptions in their own experience of caregiving, such as: parental substance misuse, family violence, limited nurturance and difficulties at school, to name just some.

Because, as Meisels and Shonkoff (2003, p. 3) eloquently put it, 'Children are the touchstone of a healthy and sustainable society', it is surely right that social pedagogic work should help children and their families to enjoy optimal well-being. At the same time, social pedagogues are committed to supporting the welfare of all human beings throughout their lives. In that respect, as Kornbeck and Rosendal Jensen (2011) make clear, the mandate of social pedagogy covers the entire lifespan. Stated forthrightly, social pedagogy is relevant for everyone, not only for young and vulnerable populations. That said, and rightly so, the poor and oppressed have an especially deserving place in the eyes of social pedagogues.

By now, it should be clear that social pedagogy sets itself the just cause of preventing and tackling social problems. Against this backdrop:

'The goal of social pedagogy is, firstly, to improve the unequal social conditions by socio-political means, and, secondly, to enable individuals to fight their own battle to improve social conditions' (Sünker & Braches-Chyrek, 2009, p. 25). It is important to note how Sünker & Braches-Chyrek position the individual as a warrior in a landscape that is bigger than her personal problems. Public issues are at stake, so individuals are enjoined to fight, with like-minded individuals, for social justice on the bigger canvas that constitutes society. As for social pedagogues, they have a double role: to change, through radical public advocacy, the social structure that produces inequality; and to assuage, via dialogic "tutoring", the pain of those who suffer social injustice by assisting them to become agents of their own destiny. Bourdieu (1999, p. 629) memorably characterises the first cause as, 'these mechanisms that make life painful, even unliveable', and the secondary manifestations as, 'unhappiness in all its forms'.

Even so, he (1999, p. 629) is optimistic because, 'what the social world has done, it can … undo'. While he understands how hard it is to eliminate or even radically modify most of the social and economic causes of the worst human suffering – particularly, the mechanisms that regulate labour and educational markets – Bourdieu (1999, p. 629) claims that political programmes which fail to take robust action against exposed injustice, 'can be considered guilty of nonassistance to a person in danger'. I think most practising social pedagogues would agree with him. I also think many of them seek to apply interventions that address simultaneously the root causes of human suffering and the personal hardships that ensue.

They know, however, that demolishing the structural basis of human suffering will take time. But this does not stop them seeking to energise collective lobbying in the cause of social justice, sometimes in the role of community organisers. Social pedagogues, as indicated earlier, also do what they can to lessen the pain of poverty and social exclusion along the way, by educating the socially disadvantaged to make beneficial decisions in life. While countless – probably, most – personal problems are strongly affected by wider social structures, I shall first examine what social pedagogic practice can achieve on the individual level before looking at the bigger picture. The reason for this is that when self-efficacy – an individual's potential – is wedded to collective resolve, the fast rolling momentum that ensues can move mountains. This is what I suspect Natorp (1904) had in mind when he wrote his illustrious book of social pedagogy on how to forge individual wills into collective determination.

Efficacy beliefs and enablement

Many readers will be acquainted with the term, "learned helplessness", which is a mental state of passivity and demoralisation and of giving up. It is a condition that has been learnt over time. However, there is a solution, and Bandura (1997) has found it in self-efficacy. Each of us possesses self-efficacy, that is, the ability to produce desired effects by our actions. However, in order to use this inherent ability, people must recognise and marshal it. When that happens, perceived self-efficacy can help them to achieve their goals (Bandura, 1997).

Because a key objective in social pedagogy is to show vulnerable people that they really can exercise more control in life, initiatives that promote perceived self-efficacy are a powerful social pedagogic tool. At this juncture, it is relevant to note that social pedagogy, like many other disciplines, applies insights derived from a range of subject areas – not least education, sociology and psychology – when these are found to produce good results. Thus, there are no formulaic techniques that are only found in social pedagogy to be put into operation. Rather, social pedagogy states its purpose – promoting advantageous social development for all – and subsequently finds the best way to accomplish this. For example, helping people to believe in their developmental capabilities is heavily reliant on optimistic 'efficacy builders' (cf. Bandura, 1997), such as social pedagogues, social workers, clinical psychologists and teachers.

It matters little which profession offers social learning tasks that provide a good chance of success. The point is that any strategy which fosters change agency and leads to life-enhancement, serves social pedagogy well. It is pertinent in this respect to reflect on a quote from von Goethe's (2001, p. 295) novel, *Wilhelm Meister's Apprenticeship*:

'When we take people merely as they are, we make them worse; when we treat them as if they were what they should be, we improve them as far as they can be improved.' The implication of Goethe's (2001) argument for social pedagogic work is that to induce latent self-efficacy is to turn resignation into hope. This does not mean that insecure people should have to stand on their own two feet. Many people are in precarious circumstances and feel unable to resolve problems on their own, even though, circumstances permitted, they might possess the inherent capacity to do so. This is why social pedagogues use enablement strategies. Typically, that entails assisting people to draw upon and develop their own capabilities by setting up optimal conditions for them to achieve goals. The emphasis is on solution building, with the right level of support to hand.

KEY QUESTION

Does my claim that it matters little what profession does good social pedagogic work, necessarily imply that anyone can be a social pedagogue?

An example of enablement is the practice, commonly used in Nordic countries, of offering people who are intellectually or physically impaired, the service of personal assistants. Social pedagogues who work in this area, provide targeted support in the form of, for example, transport, work, education, hygiene, shopping, cooking, entertainment and transport. Because the service user decides what kind of help she needs, this puts her in control and is therefore self-affirming. Promisingly, evidence from a very large randomised controlled trial in the US (Nordic Campbell Centre, 2008) suggests that personal assistance increases life quality for four main groups of people, namely:

- Children with intellectual impairments

- Adults with physical impairments

- Adults with both physical and intellectual impairments

- Older adults (65+)

Another enablement intervention is the Initiative for Women with Disabilities (Xenakis & Goldberg, 2010). This American programme enables young women aged 14 to 21 with physical disabilities to obtain access to primary care, gynaecology, physical therapy, nutritional guidance, exercise and fitness classes, and wellness and social work services. The agenda is based on a carefully planned curriculum that helps the women to apply what they learn in the programme to their everyday life. Emphasis is placed on exposing participants to experiences that foster self-care skills and self-determination, which in turn, support independent living.

The Initiative for Women with Disabilities represents a shift away from the practice of over-protecting adolescents with disabilities towards teaching them self-help strategies that promote perceived self-efficacy and the functional skills that confirm this newly gained confidence. Unwittingly, some people who "over-protect" may fail to make young disabled women aware of resources in society that foster independence, in the best sense of the word. Among the facilitating resources that need to be in place, transportation is vital (Xenakis & Goldberg, 2010). Not having accessible transport reduces supportive peer interactions with friends. This can have a negative knock-on effect because limited opportunities for healthy socialisation can lead to isolation and reduced aspirations. As well as serving young women, the Initiative for Women with Disabilities offers separate educational wellness workshops for parents and legal guardians, who play a crucial role in their children's care and development.

In the workshops, parents and guardians learn how to advocate on their daughters' behalf. Additionally, the wellness component attends to caregivers' interests and sets up a parent/guardian social network for mutual support. Social pedagogic enablement of this kind can bring needed assistance right into the service user's community. It meets people where they are rather than behind a desk in a cereal box building. While, of course, some social pedagogues work in offices, the ambulant nature of the profession ensures that social pedagogic work is also done out and about in the daily round.

Another example of enablement is the practice of acting as an advocate for persecuted people. Take, for instance, intimate partner abuse (often termed domestic violence) involving the maltreatment of a woman by a current or ex-male or ex-female partner. Advocates like social pedagogues often help people who are being abused by referring them to appropriate social, health and other services. In turn, professionals within these services commonly provide:

- Legal, housing and financial advice

- Protective shelters

- Psychological support

- Advice on safety protocols

When working with those who have much hardship in life, social pedagogues prefer dialogue to other forms of communication. A horizontal conversation is democratic and does not cast service users in the role of subordinate listeners. Indeed, dialogic interactions give voice to the Other and nurture social pedagogic empathy. Respectful communication is particularly important when the role of the social pedagogue is to foster a degree of re-socialisation. That sounds rather ominous, even doctrinaire. But the objective is benevolent, namely, to help a human being to "unlearn" despondency and to replace it with hope. In order to achieve this, habits based on "faulty" self-knowledge must be challenged. Once people have got used to believing that they have lost control, they tend to act in accordance with what they think they cannot do.

But underestimated potential does not have to be a permanent state. It has an antidote in what Bandura (1997, p. 80) calls 'enactive mastery experience'. To enact is to perform; and a mastery experience is an event that a person performs well. Even a moderately successful performance can help self-doubters to shed needless uncertainty. Furthermore, repeated success bolsters anticipatory efficacy beliefs. When a person brings a confident appraisal based on past achievements to a new challenge, she is more likely to persist in the face of difficulty. Thus the role that social pedagogues play in (re)-socialisation is of the kind described by Herrmann (2011), where the aim is not about treating deficits but nurturing development.

An effective social pedagogic method for assisting those who waver in the face of challenges is to set up a series of attainable but fairly exacting tasks. This places the social pedagogue in the role of an unobtrusive guide who helps self-doubters to gain mastery experiences by showing them how indecision is often uncalled-for. To quote Bandura (1997, p. 329):

KEY DEFINITION

'Guided mastery provides a quick and effective way of restoring reality testing. It provides disconfirming tests of phobic beliefs. But even more important, mastery experiences that are structured to develop coping skills provide persuasive confirmatory beliefs that one can exercise control over potential threats.'

In the hands of skilled and committed social pedagogues, guided mastery is a potent way of creating a resilient sense of personal efficacy. It is enacted, as indicated, by setting tasks of escalating difficulty that people are able to master on a step-by-step basis. There is no absolute guarantee of success every time, but the risk of failure can be significantly reduced if prematurely tough challenges are avoided. Even so, there will be occasions when learners fail. Before this happens, it makes good sense to prepare them for the inevitable event. One way of doing this is to explain that realistic rather than inflated performance expectations are the best option. A realistic appraisal of a task involves the contemplation and acceptance of success and failure, as well as the perception that either outcome is normal. Nobody succeeds all the time. Nobody has complete control over all situations. It is therefore reassuring for anxious social learners to understand that the worry of not being able to overcome the "uncontrollable" in life can be mitigated if they choose to exercise personal influence over controllable events (cf. Bandura, 1997).

When self-belief and hard effort do not produce desired results, social pedagogues should emphasise that determination in itself is a worthy attribute. Many of the most successful people failed a lot of times before making a breakthrough. They did not founder in the wake of failure, but kept on persevering. On a practical level, if a social pedagogue detects effort that is followed by failure, an encouraging comment might be: "You tried really hard even though you did not succeed on this occasion. But there's always tomorrow."

As noted in Chapter 2, another psychologist (and pedagogue), Jerome Bruner, has developed a theory that has quite a lot in common with Bandura's model of guided mastery. It is known as 'scaffolding' (Bruner, 1996), and its practical application can produce a robust inducement to apprehensive learners. Scaffolding is the providing of support (often in the form of a pedagogue) to novice learners in order to promote mastery experiences. As with guided mastery, scaffolding works best when achievable (but not over-simple) tasks are set and support is at hand. A "pedagogic scaffolder" judges performance potential and provides the right level of cognitive and emotional support to help the learner achieve goals through stepwise progress. In that educational role, a social pedagogue becomes an 'efficacy builder' (cf. Bandura, 1997). The objective is clear: to facilitate a learner's attempt to attain a goal that would normally be beyond his single-handed efforts – but not for long. Applying guided mastery and scaffolding (both, as indicated, closely related) into a concrete setting, I will now introduce an imagined example.

A male job-seeker in Germany wants to enter a 6-months qualification programme leading to accreditation as an assistant teacher. Successful completion of the course, which contains classroom theory and on-the-job practice, qualifies for employment in either an elementary or a high school, depending on the specialisation that he selects. The job seeker has discussed his aspiration with a social pedagogue. Her role is crucial. However, its social pedagogic force lies not in her doing all the doing, but rather supporting the job-seeker's credible ambition to take on a task. What this means in practice, is that she can "hold his hand" when needed, but she can and will let him go solo when he is confident he can do so.

Because the job-seeker wants to work in a high school, the social pedagogue proposes an assignment within realistic bounds: a talk for about 15 minutes on an interesting topic to a small group of well-behaved students. There is a fair degree of scaffolding built into this assignment, and for good reason. The job-seeker is rather apprehensive about the task. The hope is that scaffolding will offer proportionate support for the learner to try hard enough to succeed, even though he harbours a degree of self-doubt. The day of the assignment arrives and the social pedagogue has arranged for a teacher to be present during the talk. The social pedagogue will also be there. I have now moved into the present tense. The content of the presentation has already been decided by the learner, in consultation with the social pedagogue and the teacher. He is going to give a short presentation on <u>What to do in London if you are only there for a day.</u> The presenter has lived in London and he knows that the students are visiting the city on a school trip soon. So it is safe to assume that there is a common interest here.

The talk has been well-prepared. At the start, the social pedagogue and the teacher stay close to the speaker. After a few minutes, they note that things are going well and "fade out" for a while by sitting at the back of the classroom. This raises the bar. But it also signals that they have confidence in the learner even when part of the scaffolding has been carefully dismantled. The presenter continues to do a fine job and the talk ends, followed by applause from the audience. Next, comes performance feedback from the social pedagogue and the teacher. The presenter has done well and receives evaluative comments that confirm this and which bolster his perceived self-efficacy. Compliments for effort are important here. But more important is the highlighting of personal capabilities (cf. Bandura, 1997). Too much emphasis on the role of effort can, perversely, undermine the message that the learner's talents have counted the most.

Paying tribute to someone who has shown the required skills necessary to complete a learning exercise, cognitive and/or social, is foremost when working with self-doubters. In fact, even infants take pleasure in their everyday achievements. By the age of two, they can anticipate the approval or disapproval of their performance by others (Shaffer, 2009). Effort is also commended and deservedly so, even if an anxious learner fails a task. It should be added that trying hard to achieve a goal is a good predictor of success, though not necessarily on the first round.

As you will have noted, the aim of scaffolding is to put up props first and gradually remove them as progress is made. In guided mastery and scaffolding, social pedagogues praise and motivate when they see progress: "Well done! Want to try something a bit more difficult?" They also provide just enough support when needed. A hint now and then can work wonders. Offering too much support to a child or adult learner, though, can make it harder for them to make it on their own. Over time, as perceived self-efficacy strengthens, so too does resilience when problems loom. So think of the enabling of perceived self-efficacy as an investment in a person's capacity not to founder when the going gets tough. Resilience, that is, facing life's problems and refusing to give up, is one of the prizes of self-belief.

Not only does hardiness help people to bounce back after failure, it also stops them dwelling on setbacks. When he was asked about the many ideas he had in his head to make a light bulb that did not work, the American inventor, Thomas Edison (1847-1931), replied, 'I have not failed. I've just found 10,000 ways that won't work.' That is a pedagogic thought worth pondering. When social pedagogues seek to nurture resilience, persuasion is a helpful tool. If self-doubting service users can be persuaded to treat some setbacks in life as normal events, and are reminded that they have defeated problems before, then they are more likely to persevere. It is also necessary to explain to them that failure can be educative, as Edison found out. Admittedly, resilience takes time to build up, and a resolute will is necessary in order to overcome some inevitable let downs. But the upside is an increase in successes, small and few in number at first (yet still self-affirming), bigger and more frequent as confidence and accomplishment gather pace.

Another social pedagogic method that can foster perceived self-efficacy and resilience is what Bandura (1997) terms as 'instructive modelling'. In a social pedagogic setting, modelling involves the observation or visualisation of people similar to oneself performing well, and then trying out the same actions. Actually, the near-constant observing of others begins at birth and continues throughout life. Young children, especially, are particularly watchful of adult performance. If what is observed is successfully imitated, learning occurs. During instructive modelling, social pedagogues make concerted efforts to promote the imitation of helpful actions, such as effective coping behaviours. If confidence-building support is at hand, the observation of a model coping well can boost the learner's trust that she too can achieve comparable tasks. It should be added that good instructive modelling does not foster mimicry but rather intelligent (and, as appropriate, adjusted) imitation.

There are many practical ways of setting up modelling opportunities. For example, a person might be asked to observe a friend with similar capacities (but with that added extra, self-belief) coping with the same kinds of problem. This gives scope for imitation. Visualisation is another option. For instance, a social pedagogue could say, "Think of someone in similar circumstances to yourself who found solutions by joining a community action group." This thought exercise can involve a real or an imagined event. The aim, though, is to see if it works by trying it out as a mental exercise. Yet another strategy is for the social pedagogue to share some ideas on how she successfully deals with problems in her own life. Of particular importance here, is to disclose how she overcomes difficulty and how she handles failure. The next step would be to encourage the other person to borrow some relevant ideas and to act on them.

The modelling of behaviours that show how to respond to both success and failure is an important capacity-building instrument in social pedagogy. It is especially useful when working with people who avoid challenges due to feelings of personal inadequacy. Furthermore, witnessing an instructional model coping with setbacks can be just as helpful as watching a successful performance. Granted, there will be times when a service user feels so fragile that proxy action by the social pedagogue is the only course of action. It is relevant to note that such stand-in solutions are often necessary when structural arrangements (e.g. bureaucratic regulations) curb the capacity for individual agency.

KEY TASK

Set up an imagined modelling exercise, explain its social pedagogic logic, and indicate why you think it might be worth trying out.

Social pedagogues accept that the contemplation of habit change is tough if individuals feel they are on their own. Therefore, it is wise to put individuals in touch with strong-willed, self-help groups whose members believe in group welfare and shared responsibility. This is a more effective approach than to expect despondent individuals to start up their own interest groups. For as Bandura (1982, p. 143) ironically comments, 'Inveterate self-doubters are not easily forged into a collectively efficacious force'.

Collective efficacy beliefs

The mobilisation of collective efficacy beliefs is the trump card in the social pedagogic pack. This winning card is often found in cohesive communities, where people offer each other mutual support and believe that united effort can bring about beneficial social change. Perceived collective efficacy is also an effective tool in the lobbying of politicians. For while the socially disadvantaged lack political weight and economic clout, 'they have the power of numbers if their efforts are well organized and channeled' (Bandura, 1997, p. 501). Such collective sovereignty can, in turn, instigate the necessary energy for a community to improve its living conditions. There are many examples of success built upon united endeavour. By way of illustration, some years ago (the source does not provide a specific date) Elnora Yarborough organised a grassroots community initiative in her own community in Tennessee. She started alone in an effort to get a school bus to come through the neighbourhood. Before long, she had the neighbours involved in her campaign. Elnora, as can be seen, turned out to be a real fighter (Bell & Yarborough, 2003, p. 141):

> 'I guess I'll start off saying that I learned how to stand on my two feet from a school event. We had five children. During the time when they all started school, we lived on a blacktopped road and the bus was coming through. And then we bought and built on a dirt road. This particular road had quite a few kids, walking from one end to the other out to the blacktop to catch the bus. So I decided that my husband and I would go and ask the superintendent if he could put a bus through there. This was a black community. He told me no, we didn't have enough kids (in the neighborhood). I asked how many does it take. I told him I had 40. He didn't believe me.

So my husband and I got a list of the kids, and I carried it back to the superintendent. Then he thought I had made up the names. I had to go back and get the addresses and their parents' names. I went door to door, walking, and asking the parents if they would go over there in a group. Some people were scared, they had never done this before, and they didn't want to do it. So I said, we've started and we're not going to stop. I got all the information and carried it back. I had to make seven trips. I had to convince him.

Finally we got a bus – it was still a dirt road. When it was dry, the bus would come through, but when it rained, it didn't. I would have to walk out to the blacktop with coats and boots to meet the bus after school. That's when JONAH [Just Organized Neighborhoods Area Headquarters] came through, we went to fighting for a road, and we got a road.

I have learned to stand up and fight for anything in the community and anywhere. Cause all you've got to do is ask. And if they say no, don't take no for an answer. Because they're going to say no – but keep going back. You'll get something done when they know that you're a person that sticks.'

Social pedagogues can learn a great deal by listening to people like Elnora. Former Professor of Social Work and retired community worker, Bob Homan, believes that the poor need to write about their experiences. He also understands that such writing carries authentic weight (The Scottish Government, 2003). A grassroots voice is a first-hand account as opposed to a backstage report. Consequently, it gives balance to the debate. Elnora's writing is pure grassroots and it mobilised a community initiative that went on to win a glorious victory. There are, however, other forms of community action that are organised by established agencies and to which communities can turn to for support. To some extent, this represents community action by proxy, but nevertheless it still has an enabling function and should not be rebuffed. An example of such community action is found in the Northeast Florida Community Action Agency, which has been helping thousands of low-income families for more than forty years. In addition to providing financial help to needy families, the agency provides programmes that teach people to:

- earn and maintain an income

- ultimately become self-sufficient

- lead a healthy lifestyle

- lead a higher standard of living

Poor people who come to the agency bring with them a precious resource: the will to make positive changes in their lives. Social pedagogues can help them to accomplish this by taking on the role of community organisers. In this function, the social pedagogues can join existing grassroots projects or even start them up. Either way, the task is to help people to solve problems collectively that concern them in their neighbourhoods. If the main problem is poverty, a social pedagogue might organise a "door knocking" initiative in order to bring poor people together in common cause. At this point, the community organiser can pass the baton so that the poor can organise on their own behalf and for their own ends. In social pedagogic terms, this involves the enabling of grassroots action, such as the collective lobbying of local decision-makers.

The role of the social pedagogues thus becomes the "organisation of organisation". This task positions social pedagogues not as community leaders, but rather as community enablers. The goal is to assist the poor to understand that leadership is their collective asset to be used in their self-orchestrated actions to achieve social justice. In this pursuit, it is helpful to form what Lave and Wenger (2003) term 'communities of practice'. Such communities contain people who engage in collective learning, which they then apply to practice. They include, for example, individuals working and learning together to provide a more inclusive built environment for wheelchair users.

KEY QUESTION

Why does the "organisation of organisation" play a significant role in social pedagogic work?

One of the great success stories in this domain was the launching in 1989 of the American magazine, *New Mobility*. The founder, Sam Maddox, saw a community of wheelchair users who wanted more opportunities for an active lifestyle. He met that need by recruiting the service of veteran writers with disabilities to launch a magazine that would tell what living life on wheels was really like. Today, *New Mobility* promotes the inclusion of active wheelchair users into mainstream society. Moreover, the magazine has gained the respect of the disability community and professional journalists in general. This is not surprising given the perceived collective efficacy it promotes among its readers. Do have a look at the magazine by visiting its homepage on:

http://newmobility.com/index.cfm

Another example of social pedagogic practice that sets in motion collective ambitions is found in effective anti-school bullying programmes. In Norway, as referred to in Chapter 1, where some of these interventions receive government funding, the implementation of social curricula that foster esprit de corps among teachers, students and parents is crucial. The underlying social pedagogic goal of an anti-bullying initiative is to develop a school climate based on co-operation and non-violence.

KEY TASK

Suggest several social pedagogic steps that could be taken in pre-school with the goal of helping children, teachers and parents to get on well together. Indicate how your proposal endorses social pedagogic principles.

In line with the social pedagogic hopes of Natorp (1904), contemporary social pedagogues are keen to promote solidarity as a core unifying value in society. For unanimity is commensurate with shared aims in pursuit of the common good. A tried, tested and proven method for achieving positive inter-group relations is highlighted in the work of the American social psychologist, Gordon W. Allport (1897-1967). In what is generally recognised as a landmark text on racial discrimination, *The Nature of Prejudice* (1979), Allport predicted that contact between different groups would lead to a reduction in prejudice, but only if certain conditions were met.

The main conditions (Curry et al, 2010) were that members of groups should work together:

- Towards a common aim

- With interdependent roles

- With equal status

- In the context of policies that support the contact

In what is now termed the Contact Hypothesis, Allport's (1979) prediction has been found, providing all or most of the above conditions are met, to have positive effects on inter-group attitudes with a wide range of groups and in a broad variety of settings (Curry et al, 2010). While Allport was primarily concerned with inter-ethnic relations, Curry et al reported that cooperative learning strategies had a well-documented positive effect on inter-group (including inter-ethnic) relations among children. This finding should encourage social pedagogues to promote, even engineer, increased interactions between different groups in society under favourable conditions. For example, bringing minority groups together through cultural events such as music, theatre and food might produce some of the positive effects that are predicted in the Contact Hypothesis. If this happens, there are benefits for a whole community, not least. enhanced feelings of friendship and solidarity.

Seeking to bring about positive change on the community or societal plane is always going to be a demanding task. This is because vested interests and entrenched narrow attitudes, often perpetuated by local and national elites, are tough nuts to crack. In such circumstances, the illusion of personal autonomy on the part of the service user – sometimes peddled as rugged individualism – is just that, an illusion. The truth is that unjust social structures tend to crush individual agency. Notwithstanding, social pedagogues are adept at finding ways of gaining some measure of influence over macro-level policymaking.

Macro-level decisions and micro-level solutions

Macro-level decisions are made at the highest levels of society. They typically involve the pronouncements of those at the pinnacle of power. Politicians, corporate executives, trade union bosses and top military brass are among the elites who occupy these heights. Often, the decisions of a handful of men (and they usually are men!) bear heavily upon social policymaking. In this section, my interest is in the politicians who make major social policy decisions, often with catastrophic results, and the care professionals who seek to find solutions to social problems on the micro- level of society. Social pedagogues, whose task it is to relieve the pain of people whose lives are full of suffering, know that much of the immediate problem is symptomatic of wrong decisions at the top.

They also understand that the only way to remedy society's ills is to bring about more continuity between welfare policy on the macro-(or state) level and the capacity for professional judgement on the micro- (or carer-user) level. If this connection is absent or weak, even the most committed social pedagogues will butt their heads against an all too powerful polity. Bourdieu (2004) highlights the dilemma in his analysis of the relationship between the Right Hand and the Left Hand of the French State. The Left Hand (broadly understood to cover 'social workers' that include, for example, teachers, rank-and-file magistrates and youth leaders) confronts the Right Hand (the polity and banks) at every twist and turn. But this not a fair fight. The Right Hand has political and economic muscle on its side, the Left Hand a dream rooted in emancipatory aims.

Nevertheless, social workers are sent into the front line to compensate for the harsh austerity of the market without being given the tools to do the job (Bourdieu, 2004). Furthermore, care professionals in France and elsewhere are witnesses to circumstances in which "ordinary" people – and especially the poor – are disrespected, crushed and turned into passive spectators of their own misfortune (cf. Freire, 2007).

KEY TASK

Put Bourdieu's (2004) argument regarding the Right Hand and the Left Hand of the French State into more simple terminology. Use concrete or imagined examples if you wish.

Bourdieu's (2004) depiction of the French experience is an example of a "loggerheads" model, where politicians and care professionals have different agendas. But it does not have to be this way. In Norway, for example, a united commitment to universal welfare is the norm in policymaking and practice settings. What this means, is that the macro-level enablement of micro-level solutions actually happens. Consider the Nordic model of early childhood education and care (ECEC). All the Nordic welfare states (Denmark, Finland, Iceland, Norway and Sweden) operate a fully integrated ECEC system. This means that there is universal entitlement for children from at least 12 months old, a single funding system and a single workforce based on graduate early years professionals who work directly with children (Moss, 2010).

The ECEC system rescues the Nordic countries from what Moss (2010, no pagination) refers to as a 'dysfunctional jumble of services'. For example, Nordic welfare makes it easier for dual-earner and lone parent earner families to enter or remain in paid employment, thereby increasing family income. The consequence is a macro-level structural arrangement that facilitates a micro-level solution, namely, earning a pay cheque. No wonder UK policymakers are interested in obtaining more knowledge about social pedagogic practice in the Nordic countries. One lesson they could learn from the Nordic model(s) is that for a welfare state to function well, it needs to be purposive and comprehensive, not reluctant and residual.

Looking at Norway specifically, the government there has set out policy decisions in a document that mandates the main professional route for social pedagogic education and training. This document – the *National Framework and Regulations for the 3-Year Education of Child Welfare Pedagogues* (Norwegian Ministry of Education and Norwegian Ministry of Children & Families, 2005, p. 17) – explicitly states that social pedagogues should critique societal problems:

> 'To be able to influence societal development, it is necessary to know about mechanisms and processes in society that create inequality, as well as having a critical view of society.'

This is a political document that invites social pedagogues to critique aspects of government policy. Such influence over political decision-making is rare in most countries, where governments prefer to keep their deliberations within the higher circles. The elites might be distracted by debating publics, such as caring professions, but they are rarely trumped by them. Even so, social pedagogic practitioners have a knack of finding and getting into awkward nooks and crannies. This dexterity is heavily reliant on the ambulant nature of the profession. More than most care professionals, social pedagogues meet people in the daily round: in homes, on the streets, in community clubs, in schools, even in prisons. That outreach mobility is de-institutionalised from the casework office where "experts" and "clients" meet impersonally. I think that Buber's (2004, p. 39) observation that, 'Feelings are "within", where life is lived and man recovers from institutions', captures the essence of a social pedagogic encounter in a setting outside an office.

Closing the distance between the social pedagogue and the service user gives meaning to Mill's (2000) assertion that private troubles and public issues are inter-connected. This entails looking at the bigger picture in the relationship between the individual and society. The aim is to understand the service user's total (or holistic) situation rather than fragments of individual life histories. By adopting this perspective, social pedagogues are able to identify (and sometimes even remedy to a limited extent) first causes of social problems in society before dealing with these secondly, in their symptoms.

Advocacy work of this kind builds on the legacy of Grace Abbott (1860-1935), whose community engagement in Chicago brought her close to the people she served, and a Nobel Peace Prize along the way in 1931. Abbott's example inspires any social worker or social pedagogue who sees herself as a champion of human rights and social justice, whatever her job-description. Such conviction engages professional work of the kind that changes private and community lives for the better. Sometimes this is done within legislative frameworks (e.g. social services) and sometimes outside of these structures (e.g. charitable organisations). Either way, the goal is (or should be) unified effort in the pursuit of socially just outcomes.

Even though compared to other nations, the Nordic countries have arguably paid more attention to the impact of societal factors on a population's well-being, it is reassuring to see that the World Health Organization (WHO), is pressing governments to take more cognisance of these issues. Indeed WHO (2003, p. 13) is on record as stating that:

> 'Governments should recognize that welfare programmes need to address both psychosocial and material needs: both are sources of anxiety and insecurity. In particular, governments should support families with young children, encourage community activity, combat social isolation, reduce material and financial insecurity, and promote coping skills in education and rehabilitation.'

Health policy used to be thought of as little more than the funding and providing of medical care. Thankfully, this view has changed. The health of a nation is now known to be crucially affected by economic and social circumstances that make people ill in the first place (Wilkinson & Marmot, 2003, in WHO, 2003). Consider, for example, the city of Glasgow. People there who live in the poorest districts have a life expectancy 12 years less than those in the most affluent districts (Marmot, 2006). Per Fugelli (2011, p. 3), a Norwegian professor of social medicine, has provided a succinct summary of the policy implications of Wilkinson's and Marmot's pioneering work in the field of health inequality:

- The need for redistributive social policies that are mindful of income inequalities.

- The need for stronger universal arrangements in sectors such as health, education and benefits.

It is noteworthy that Fugelli is from Norway, a country popularly dubbed a "Milton Friedman Free-Zone". So his political vision is likely to be broadly in line with the views of many politicians in the country. It remains to be seen if nations such as the UK – which has a welfare state containing universal and neo-liberal elements, but increasingly weighted towards the latter – will take up the challenge of creating a socially just society. If they do, they will create the necessary structural conditions for social pedagogic work to flourish. For social pedagogues need enablement too, in this case, a society that guarantees a social contract with all the people. Only by anchoring her work in the service user's "total life" in society, can the social pedagogue achieve optimal professional success. This involves assisting individuals to "relearn" (in the sense of improving) aspects of their lives in a welfare state based on comprehensive social citizenship (cf. Andersen, 2002). The so-called Scandinavian model of welfare provides just such a setting.

KEY QUESTION

What can social policymakers learn from social pedagogy about the characteristics of an effective and a just welfare state?

Concluding remarks

By way of conclusion, it is useful to look briefly at a study by Petrie et al (2006) of social pedagogic work with children in care in Continental Europe. This important comparative research prompted the researchers to deduce that good social pedagogic practice requires the juxtaposing of "heart", "head" and "hands". That is a delicate balance and one which requires human warmth, rationality and practical activities. There are allusions here to Pestalozzi's reform pedagogy, in which heart, head and hands uphold an education of the whole child. In work with children, out of this union emerges a distinguishing feature of compassionate social pedagogic practice: the capacity to become a secure adult base in a child's life. The term 'secure base' comes from psychoanalytic theory (cf. Bowlby, 2005), and personifies a relationship in which the child can turn to a significant and trusted adult for emotional sanctuary and support.

Regardless of whether social pedagogues do their work in child welfare, schools, disability care or in other fields, they frequently do battle with feelings of despondency among people who have given up trying because of self-doubt. This is why social pedagogues who are able to re-kindle staying power and hope attain the highest reaches of their profession. In the next chapter, I shall explore values in social pedagogic helping relationships.

Chapter 4
Social Pedagogic Values

'[T]he moral sense or conscience .... is the most noble of all the attributes of man, leading him without a moment's hesitation to risk his life for that of a fellow-creature; or after due deliberation, impelled simply by the deep feeling of right or duty, to sacrifice it in some great cause' (Charles Darwin,1874; republished 2007, p. 85).

Introduction

In this chapter, I examine social pedagogic values. As made clear earlier, social pedagogy does not take a neutral position on societal issues. Far from it, the moral aim of social pedagogic practice is to contribute to the development of a socially just society in which all people can develop their full potential. Emancipatory social pedagogic practice is on the side of the oppressed and for social justice. Like Darwin's salute to a noble conscience (2007), it celebrates selfless altruism.

There are different categories of value; some are relatively distinct, while others tend to overlap. Examples of values in general include aesthetic values, consumption values and kinship values. For present purposes, my concern is with ethical values, that is to say, beliefs about right and wrong. Compassion is the signature value of social pedagogy, at least in contemporary Europe. Being compassionate is a dependable guarantor of what Bauman (2009, p. 11) describes as, 'answerability to the Other' – in this case, the needy. Even so, few guarantees are unwavering, and there have been instances when social pedagogy has been used for malign purposes. A terrible illustration of this was the misuse of social pedagogy by so-called National Socialists (the German version of fascism) to instil Nazi values (cf. Sünker & Otto, H.-U., 1997).

KEY QUESTIONS

What criticism might be levelled at my assertion that social pedagogy can be used for benign or malign aims? How would you reply to such criticism?

This disturbing case is a timely reminder that disciplinary knowledge can be used for different purposes. Consider physics, for instance. The discipline has been applied constructively (e.g., in medical diagnosis and treatment) and destructively (e.g., to produce cluster bombs). Similarly, social pedagogy has been practised for good (e.g., to reduce bullying in schools) and for ill (e.g., to inculcate racist ideology, as in the Nazi celebration of "das Deutsche Volk"). It also happens that humane efforts have been thwarted in the social professions, a process documented by Reisch and Andrews (2002) in their aptly titled book, *The Road not Taken*. The reader is reminded of a time when social workers with radical ideas were assailed by politicians and the press, hassled by the FBI and the House Un-American Committee, and even sacked. On a more upbeat note, the muting of critical voices was hard to pull off. This is why American social workers are still 'asking "forbidden" questions' about the intransience of poverty and the real meaning of equality and democracy (Reisch & Andrews, 2002, p. 230).

In that frame of mind, the American political philosopher, Iris Marion Young (2011), takes up the challenge of moral accountability in her critique of structural injustice in the US. Young (2011) argues that the presence of injustice begs the question, Who is responsible? Her answer is, 'that all those who contribute by their actions to structural processes with some unjust outcomes share responsibility for the injustice' (Young, 2011, p. 96). It follows, says Young, that those who participate in structural actions which produce unjust outcomes, bear a moral responsibility to make good. The exercise of compassionate social pedagogic practice in an unjust society is a moral imperative. But it calls forth inventiveness, dedication and courage. These rare qualities were personified in the legendary Grace Abbott (referred to earlier in this book), who became a social worker in 1908, and worked with immigrants at the Hull House in Chicago. Her unflagging compassion was given especially to new immigrants, the so-called hyphenated Americans, such as Irish-Americans and Chinese-Americans. Abbott (1917) recognised the contributions that immigrants made to America and lamented 'The tyranny' of 'Undiluted Americanism' (ibid., p. 271).

In this, she was well ahead of her time. Abbott was also a notable figure in the struggle for federal legislation to protect children's rights. In that field, she played a leading role in the passing of the Sheppard-Towner Act in 1921, which coordinated federal and state aid for mothers and children. Not short on radical and compassionate ideals, Abbott also supported the idea of a permanent and well-funded national relief programme. In the history of American social work, few have matched Abbott's achievements. This is woeful but not surprising, given the strong anti-social work sentiments that prevail in neo-liberal US policymaking.

KEY QUESTION

Would it be fair to argue that Grace Abbott was both a social worker and a social pedagogue?

Lakoff (2002) has conceptualised that antipathy in his metaphor of a Strict Father Morality in American politics. In this brand of extreme conservatism, the poor are coddled by the dole, while the rich scurry up the Ladder of Opportunity. Not everyone is persuaded by this account. Mills (1973, p.348), for example, disputes, 'the proud claim of the higher circles in America that their members are entirely self-made'. That illusion, says Mills (ibid., p. 348), 'is their self-image and their well-publicized myth'. For all that, elite myths are hard to shift, and this particular myth serves the peddlers of the Blame Game well. On that account, personal failure rather than social injustice is seen as the primary cause of poverty and other social problems. However, there is a flaw here, not to mention an insult. The Strict Father Morality policymakers conjure up an image of a level playing field, in which societal arrangements are essentially fair, not stacked against the poor (cf. Young, 2011). The fact, of course, is the very opposite.

But that does not stop Strict Father Morality politics prevailing on Capitol Hill, nor the raft of "get tough, stand on your own two feet" welfare policies which follow. The ironic and tragic outcome of these policies (most of which advocate Workfare interventions) is the transition of the 'welfare poor' into the 'working poor' (cf. Schram, 2006). The fiction of a level playing field must be challenged in the institutions that run social services and also in public forums. Social pedagogues are well placed to launch the challenge, a point I shall address in this chapter.

KEY QUESTION

With reference to Lakoff's (2002) metaphor of Strict Father Morality in American politics, to what extent if any is this conception relevant to welfare politics in Britain or any other nation that you are familiar with?

The nature of compassion

Before considering compassion in social pedagogic work, it is necessary to understand what the virtue entails. Father Florenzo Maria Rigoni's formulation of, 'compassion as a sister to empathy, a feeling together, a perception that the other person's world is partly my world too' (2007, p. 19), captures the spirit. For this reason, it inspires a fitting (paraphrased) definition for that virtue:

KEY DEFINITION

Compassion is the companion of empathy. It constitutes a feeling of togetherness, a sense that the Other's world is part of my world, as well.

This kind priest shares the pain of unwanted migrants, giving solace in no-name dealings with the undocumented. Although he is not, formally speaking, a social pedagogue, Fr. Rigoni's unremitting care of the Other is in the best tradition of social pedagogic work. In African philosophy, there is a particular kind of compassion known as *ubuntu* (Tuto, in King, 2007, p.3). Archbishop Tuto (ibid., p.3) explains that 'this wonderful quality' is present in the, 'person [who] treats others as he or she would be treated'. Fr. Rigoni has *ubuntu*, and it flows over. His is a model of kind-heartedness worthy of imitation. The universal ethic of *ubuntu* is found in all major religions. In the Christian religion, it is known as the Golden Rule: 'Do unto others as you would have others do unto you' (Matthew 7, 12).

The Golden Rule calls attention to the moral connectedness of human beings. In strong community settings – for example, coal mining towns – a sense of esprit de corps can be so intense that people are willing to suffer with, even for, those who face the most severe hardships. This is because the local community works for the common good, just as a genuinely universal welfare state (are there any though?) does for the benefit of all. In philosophy, there are clear parallels between the Golden Rule and Immanuel Kant's (1724-1804) Categorical Imperative. Kant (1993, p. 14) expounded his famous Imperative as follows:

'I should never act except in such a way that I can also will that my maxim should become a universal law'.

Conceded, there are debates concerning alleged similarities between the Golden Rule and the Categorical Imperative. Nevertheless, both principles support the ethic of social justice. This ethic, which goes hand-in-hand with compassion, is understood as fairness for all by the American philosopher, John Rawls (2003), earlier referred to. In his celebrated book, *A Theory of Justice*, Rawls (2003, p. 6) explains that, 'Our topic, however, is that of social justice.' By this, he indicates that he is more interested in the social as opposed to the legal dimensions of justice. Although notions of social justice are arguably contingent on particular contexts, Rawls (2003) constructs a pure type at a high level of analytical abstraction. There are echoes of Plato here. The setting of this unblemished model is an imagined 'Original Position' of equality.

From that primordial beginning – conceptual, not real – equals would face the task of reaching agreement about the true nature of social justice. To do so, they would have to agree on how to divide basic assets, such as rights, liberties, opportunities, income and wealth. Because, though, they do not know their place in society nor their assets, these hypothetical equals would be unable to customise rights to their particular advantage. They would instead have to conduct their deliberations in a state of collective amnesia. Rawls (2003) also assumes that the parties would accept that the principles finally agreed upon would be respected by all. This pre-supposes a common understanding of fair play. In these circumstances, Rawls believes it would be theoretically possible to reach agreement and act upon a conception of social justice. So what then is that conception?

He concludes that, because it would not be reasonable for any one individual to expect more nor less than an equal share of available assets, the idea of social justice as a call for equal shares would appeal to all parties. Thus, in its pure form, social justice would be understood as a principle that grants equal rights and liberties, equality of opportunity and an equal division of income and wealth.

KEY DEFINITION

Rawls (2003) conceives of social justice as a principle that confers equal human rights and freedoms, equality of opportunity and an equal share of income and wealth.

Because *A Theory of Justice* tends to attract readers who are familiar with philosophical argumentation, Rawls's (2003) writing style is highly academic. For that reason, I invite my students to participate in a group thought exercise (about five students per group) which is broadly based on my interpretation of Rawl's Original Position. Most of them do not have a strong background in philosophy, but the task helps them to grasp the essence of the concept. It is important to bear in mind that the task addresses an imagined, primordial, uncorrupted world. The intention is not to take it literally or to apply it on a real operational level. That said, it might inspire some fresh Big Ideas among those who work or who are going to work with socially disadvantaged people.

An Adapted Rawlsian Thought Exercise

Imagine you wake up one day on a beautiful South Pacific island. You find yourself in the company of four other people. All of you are young, fit and healthy, and equal in every other respect. None of you know each other. Moreover, due to temporary amnesia, you have forgotten your previous life histories and, consequently, what you once valued. You do not remember your previous social backgrounds either. But you all know that to survive, you need food, water and shelter. On the island, there are five luxurious houses spaced 50 metres apart, each with equally grand views and each enjoying close proximity to fresh drinking water and an abundance of fresh fruit and vegetables. These resources are at your collective disposal.

Your task is to reach unanimous agreement, if you can, on how to allocate the available resources fairly. Please justify your final decision(s).

On the several occasions that the students have performed this exercise, about 80 per cent of them concluded that the resources should be shared equally. They believed this was a fair course of action. Rawls (2003), it should be emphasised, treats "fair" as a synonym for "just". The students who reached unanimity did so from behind a so-called veil of ignorance; that is to say, they had no recollection of their previous life histories. The findings carry no empirical veracity, but the results do not surprise me. Moreover, empirical evidence shows that, when people are asked about the meaning of fairness in relation to various practical issues, quite stable patterns of belief are generally evident (Miller, 1999).

Enthrallingly, the thought exercise removes the dilemma of opting for the lesser evil. The only "moral logic" is to choose between right or wrong. If I had taken part in the assignment, I would have said that the allocation of equal shares is the only fair choice. At the very least, this means that I must not violate the rights of another human being, which is a kind of default position. At best, my belief implies that I should follow the

Golden Rule by treating other people as I would have them treat me. In other words, I am obliged to act compassionately.

KEY TASK

If you can get a group together, have a go at the *Adapted Rawlsian Thought Exercise* that I have set my social pedagogy students in Norway.

While Rawls (2003) thinks that human beings – or at least, most of them – have an intuitive attachment to the primacy of social justice, he assumes that free and rational persons would accept *his* version of social justice if they were in the Original Position. He might be right, but the assumption is based on role play in an imagined universe of philosophers.

Notwithstanding, Rawls contends that the well-being of others is actually necessary (and evident) for the well-being of everyone. In short, he believes that people really do accept the conditions embodied in the Original Position; and if we do not, says Rawls (2003, p.514), 'then we can be persuaded to do so by philosophical considerations …'

KEY TASK

Assess the proposition that Rawls's (2003) conception of social justice is broadly congruent with the social pedagogic goal of developing a society based on Gemeinschaft values.

With regard to social pedagogic practice, fairness means treating the least advantaged befittingly according to their needs. It deserves mention that these needs are usually no different from those of human beings in general, a point convincingly argued by Lewis (2003, pp. 15-16):

'In their normal state, persons seeking help do not differ markedly from the general population in the personal interests they wish to satisfy. While individuals may differ in their ordering and intensity of interests, they do not differ in their desire to experience security, health, justice, knowledge, self-fulfilment, and aesthetic satisfactions.' Sadly, Lewis's (2003) itinerary of justifiable hopes is usually thwarted because policy actions to eliminate poverty are either feeble or absent in most societies. Only the politics of distributive justice would give the poor enough of society's economic pie to lift them out of poverty. But the political will is not there, nor do the rich want to share their wealth. This is why social pedagogues must tackle poverty unflinchingly. That very goal stimulated the work of one of the most brilliant and influential 20th century pedagogues, Paulo Freire.

Freire (1996a; 1996b; 2006; 2007), saw education as a vehicle for the learning and practice of social justice. His work began in efforts to promote adult literacy for the socially disadvantaged prior to the military coup of 1964 in Brazil. That event would soon lead to his exile from the country. Freire had a fulsome view of pedagogy in which social learning (and thus, implicitly, social pedagogy) was prominent. He supported a 'pedagogy of the oppressed' that fostered the development of "conscientização" (Portuguese: critical consciousness) and democracy. In this pedagogy, reading and writing were crucial; and so too was semantic critique. For in critique, the poor would understand the reality and nature of oppression and how to overcome it. Why, for example, call a man who exploits you "senhor" (Portuguese) when "opressor" (Portuguese) is a more fitting description? Problematizing questions like this are designed to help those who have been "diminished" by myths about their own inferiority. The myth creators are elites who do not want the poor to think. Others will do that for them:

'The elite defend a *sui generis* democracy, in which the people are "unwell" and require "medicine" – whereas in fact their "ailment" is the wish to speak up and participate' (Freire, 2007, p. 11).

Through the Adult Education Project of the Movement of Popular Culture in Recife, Brazil (of which Freire was Coordinator), Freire and his colleagues set up a so-called 'culture circle'. In the circle, coordinators replaced teachers; dialogue replaced lectures; group participants replaced pupils; and compact programme units replaced curricula. This innovative model of pedagogy expanded in Brazil, with debate and dialogue taking over some forms of rote instruction. Importantly, the group also decided what to debate. Social issues were prominent and included democracy and the role of illiterate people (Freire, 2007).

This was the launch of a Promethean project: the social pedagogisation of the poor in Brazil so that they might become Subjects rather than Objects of History. Freire's critical literacy programme would prove to be highly successful in the early 1960s. Not only did illiterate agricultural and industrial workers learn to read and write in rapid time, they also learnt, semantically speaking, to "re-write" the world in a way that would humanise it. This gave teachers a new role; they were to become cultural workers who would "teach", "learn" and practise democracy together with the oppressed, and never tire of doing so (cf. Freire, 1996b). The role resonates with the social pedagogic principle of working for and with communities by encouraging individuals, as collective agents, to have more voice in local decision-making rather than leaving matters to the proxy decrees of politicians.

One of my students recently asked me if Freire's 'pedagogy of the oppressed' was relevant to social pedagogic work in a relatively egalitarian society, like Norway. What a good question! I explained that consciousness raising among the socially disadvantaged is the raison d'être of social pedagogy in any country. True, income inequalities are harsher in Brazil than in Norway. But oppressed groups are still found in both countries: for example, black people in Brazil and asylum seekers in Norway.

One could, I suppose, debate gradations of subjugation in different nations. But then I must pose the question, Should any level of oppression be tolerated? Karl Kraus (cited by Bourdieu, 2004, pp. 8-9), memorably remarked, 'between two evils, I refuse to choose the lesser'. It follows that less oppression can only be less bad, but never noble.

KEY QUESTION

How would you reply to the following question: Is Freire's 'pedagogy of the oppressed' relevant to social pedagogic work in the society in which you live?

The idea of achieving something "less bad" might, at times, sound realistic, but it should not dissuade social policymakers from vigorously pursuing ethical politics. In Norway, for example, Parliament has produced an explicitly ethical document that sets out the national criteria for the 3-year Bachelor degree in Child Welfare Pedagogy (Utdannings- og forskningsdepartementet, 2005). I briefly referred to this important policy document earlier. The course prepares students for social pedagogic work with children and their families, though not all graduates work in child services. Some choose to work in after-school clubs, educational psychology services, prisons and adult psychiatry.

The document in question affirms that social pedagogy underpins the preparation of child welfare pedagogues. It also articulates social welfare values, as enunciated by the political compilers of the course specifications (which can, within certain limits, be interpreted and adjusted by course providers). Notable among these values, are the following:

- Social justice

- Helping/caring for others

- Human dignity

- Empathy

- Solidarity

- Service user participation

- Social critique

- Good communication

- Confidence-building

- Change agency

(Stephens, 2011b)

It is reassuring that social critique is valued in the criteria for the education of child welfare pedagogues. The politicians in Oslo have also made it clear that, in a good society, people (especially welfare professionals) must take care of each other (cf. Etzioni, 2002). This shows that, as policymakers, they are willing to be held to a high standard in health and social policy. In Norway, this means that needy populations must be offered, 'something more than sheer survival: survival with dignity…' (Bauman, 2007, p. 45). The Nordic way, which has strong citizen support, endorses generous welfare provision. In addition, the Norwegian government accepts that it has a moral obligation to eradicate poverty (Royal Norwegian Ministry of Labour and Social Inclusion, 2009).

This readiness to bring social justice into the arena of political decision-making stands in stark contrast to leaner welfare regimes, such as the US, where personal obligation is seen as more important than public sector accountability. I think that the Nordic welfare model has got its moral priorities right.

The case for compassion in social pedagogy

The primary ethical obligation of social pedagogic practice is to enhance the well-being of everyone, and especially people who are socially disadvantaged. Lewis (2003, p. 27) states this duty succinctly:

'In simple terms, if the client is hungry, feed him; if he is freezing, clothe him; if he is homeless, shelter him.' The justification for this ethic of compassionate care in the social professions can be found in the great biblical and philosophical texts, and are so familiar they hardly require further declaration. To act compassionately, need not be (and generally is not) based on rational justification, because compassion seldom presents itself to the court of logic. If knowledge could move the heart through reason alone, there would be no need for humanitarian social pedagogy.

This is not to suggest that, in its documentation of social problems, social pedagogy should shy away for being objective, rational and impartial. On the contrary, empirical evidence and robust argumentation highlight and critique many forms of social suffering. But once this knowledge is reliably obtained, a moral judgment must be made: either to do nothing by being indifferent *or* to do something by acting for the common good. The essence of this dilemma is captured in a famous quote that is sometimes, but erroneously, attributed to the Irish philosopher, Edmund Burke (1729-1797):

'The only thing necessary for the triumph of evil is for good men to do nothing' (source unknown).

What Burke actually wrote, in 1770 (p. 106), was:

'When bad men combine, the good must associate; else they will fall, one by one, an unpitied sacrifice in a contemptible struggle'.

The two quotations convey an unequivocal message. When social injustice occurs, social pedagogues are morally bound to right this wrong as far as they can through effective and compassionate practice. The remedy is rooted in well-informed, kind-hearted, personal work with socially disadvantaged people, and also in the wider social pedagogic goal of seeking to build a just society. In that regard, it is appropriate to reassert that personal troubles and public issues are usually linked (cf. Mills, 2000). But even though individual hardship is typically rooted in an unjust social structure, much can be done in the relationship between the social pedagogue and the service user. I am inspired here by Bauman, who in the Foreword to his book, *Liquid Love* (2003, p. viii), writes:

'The principal hero of this book is human *relationship*…. and particularly being related "for good".'

In a neo-liberal world that portrays welfare recipients as malingerers or work-shy, it is uplifting that social pedagogues refuse to apportion undeserved blame on people whose lives are too hard to bear. Instead, they choose to show compassion and offer encouragement to those whom they serve. A moral stand can be taken ex nihilo here, being its own and sufficient reason (cf. Bauman, 2009). In this spirit, it is surely right that social pedagogues are committed to eliminating (or at least, reducing) the personal pain that many service users endure. In part, that involves educating people to advocate for their own needs and rights by stimulating perceived self-efficacy. In her face-to-face dealings with services users, the social pedagogue offers a safe haven (namely, a secure base, cf. Bowlby, 2005) to whom they can turn for gentle reassurance and kind support. This is not always easy and, at times, the social pedagogue must find ways of salvaging compassionate practice (cf. Lipsky, 1980). Yet even small triumphs bring vicarious joy because "being-for-the-Other" means sharing the prize.

Offering social pedagogic "first aid" to a distraught service user is necessary, but there is also work to be done on the macro-level because political elites tend to assume that (the rest of) society can take personal suffering in its stride. The social pedagogic response is to engage in advocacy work in various institutional hierarchies. The aim is to remind the policymakers that personal pain does matter and can be remedied. For example, a social pedagogue might use her professional skills to tackle a problem that has arisen because a public body has failed in its duty of care to a service user. She will probably need to liaise with senior administrators in order to find a solution. There are various possible outcomes. Resolving the immediate difficulty would be a good start. But there is also an opportunity for institutional learning; in this case, how to learn from the mistake and ensure it does not happen again. If this leads to new practice guidelines, that in itself would be a structural-level change – small, to be sure, but nevertheless significant.

On a bigger canvas, social pedagogic work in the cause of a more just society often entails efforts to influence the political system. The task is a challenging one, but the social pedagogue is an expert at the double-bind. She sees personal tragedy at close quarters, yet does not blame the victim. Instead, like Mills (1973, p. 343), she knows that the first causes of social suffering typically arise from 'problems of *structural* immorality'. From this perspective, 'pursuit of the moneyed life is the commanding value, in relation to which the influence of other values has declined (Mills, 1973, p. 346).' The outcome is ruthless policymaking that maintains, even widens, economic inequality. The political culprits need to be reminded that high public office demands, 'equal concern for the fate of every person over whom [they claim] dominion' (Dworkin, 2011, p.2). And who is there to remind them? Social pedagogues who understand, along with Bourdieu (1999, p. 629), 'that nothing is less innocent than noninterference'.

KEY QUESTION

How do you interpret Bourdieu's (1999) assertion above?

There are many ways of bringing to the attention of politicians the message that they could be doing much more to help the socially disadvantaged. These include direct persuasion, evidence supplied to legislative committees and speaking up at public hearings. Direct lobbying is another strategy, and can be especially effective if politicians have patently reneged on campaign promises. The task has been made easier by a new piece of software, the so-called "Change Tracker" tool, which monitors policy promises on public policy websites. If, for example, a mayor has publicly pledged on a City Hall website to fund more respite care for lone parents, a website tracker can be used to see if the promise has been kept. Used in this way, the tracker functions as an electronic (and moral) "watchdog".

As is well known, disparities between political rhetoric and action are commonplace. Speechmaking is for display; policy is what happens. And never the twain shall meet, as Rudyard Kipling would have added. If campaign promises are not upheld, particularly those involving measures that offer hope for the poor, social pedagogues must challenge politicians not to go back on their word. This should be done, whenever possible, in public forums. Such forums also provide a chance to put the moral case for incorporating social justice into welfare legislation.

Given that social pedagogues are the servants of service users rather than government departments, they should also consider taking grassroots action in the pursuit of socially just politics. This course of action can gain significant impetus if coalitions are formed with service users, trade unions and other interest groups who are ready to contest political decisions that create structural hardship for the socially disadvantaged.

Big Tent alliances can then flex collective muscle by pooling resources and taking collective action in common cause.

Social pedagogic lobbying on the structural level ultimately represents a call for distributive justice, namely, fair allocation of resources according to human need. If this entreaty is unheeded in social policy circles, 'the caring role of [social work] will continue to be sabotaged by overwhelming deprivations' (Lewis, 2003, p. 216). It is important to note that distributive justice is based on two fundamental principles:

i) like shares, all else being equal (one child, one cookie)

ii) proportionate shares if needs vary (feed the hungry first)

No society acts optimally on these values, but some societies get closer to the goal than others. The work of the Danish sociologist, Gøsta Esping-Andersen (2004), is particularly important here. According to him (2004), Nordic welfare states are more likely to have the most universal welfare services. This is because the Nordic welfare model is based on social democratic values that crowd out the market and rally universal solidarity. It is form of welfare also known for being 'vocally committed to equalize living conditions across the citizenry' (Esping-Anderson & Myles, no date; no pagination).

Left-of-centre political and trade union leaders from Denmark, Finland, Iceland, Norway and Sweden were recently given the opportunity to express their views on the Nordic model of society in a Norwegian national newspaper (Stoltenberg et al, 31 January 2012). The authors produced a joint news article. Here are some of the key points:

- Most comparative studies show that the best place in the world to grow up and live in is a Nordic country.

- The Nordic model promotes economic growth with equality. This, in turn, has led to a high degree of political legitimacy and a strong voice for the people in decision-making.

- The Nordic model rests on three core principles: equal opportunities; social solidarity; and security for all.

- Nordic welfare is essentially universal and follows the principle of distributive justice in the allocation of public assets.

- Investment in services for children and older people have made it possible for women to work and to enter political arenas.

- The future of the Nordic welfare model must be secured through collective efforts involving investment in social scientific research, an improved education system and more opportunities for learning throughout the life cycle.

KEY TASK

Consider the above Nordic "inventory" systematically. Then consider any similarities and differences between that model of society and the model of society in the country where you live.

Rhetoric aside, Nordic countries do, in fact, tend to implement the most redistributive economic policies (Esping-Anderson & Myles, no date; no pagination). On the Rawlsian criterion of social justice – that is, sharing the cake more fairly – this indicates that Nordic nations are doing relatively well compared to other welfare regimes. Thus the Nordic way is more in touch with social pedagogic values and aims, which, in turn, means potentially less tension between welfare policy intentions and welfare practice. Be that as it may, there is still much to be done in Northern Europe, just as there is (and usually more) elsewhere.

I am under no illusion that the task facing social pedagogues who try to bring social justice into social policy is an undertaking of biblical proportions. David versus Goliath comes to mind. So does the fact that David won. Moreover, all institutional arrangements have chinks in their armour, and a resourceful social pedagogue is adept at finding them. It is also heartening to heed Bourdieu's (1999, p. 629) optimistic belief that making known the social origins of human suffering is cause for celebration because, 'what the social world has done, it can, armed with this knowledge, undo'. The unknotting of social injustice starts and ends with a policy commitment to distributive justice. That project, were it to succeed, would eliminate the need for many social interventions. Thus, for example, a fair division of economic resources in the UK, would eradicate poverty in a stroke. Moreover, a nation without poverty would be a nation with far less collateral suffering, such as homelessness, malnutrition and ill-health. Were it so!

The reality today (which, don't forget, could be "undone"!) is that many rich nations spend vast amounts of public revenue on the military, the result being cuts in social programmes and increases in social problems (Lewis, 2003, p. 216). Consider the US. This, the richest nation in the world, spent 800 billion dollars on the most recent war in Iraq, which "ended" in late 2011. Think how that money could otherwise have been used. The problem of prioritising "guns" over "butter" is further compounded by fiscal policies that under-tax the rich and over-tax those on low incomes. Therein is the root cause of social oppression: a society whose leaders have given up on, if they ever believed in, social justice.

I understand those who think that the goal of eliminating structural injustice is much easier said than done. Notwithstanding, history shows that **it** – changing a status quo – really can be done. If effectively mobilised, collective conviction can rouse a march of history and lead to radical social change. This is evidenced, for example, by the revolutionary struggle in South Africa, which led to the abolition of apartheid and the presidency of Nelson Mandela. In most cases, of course, changes in social structure are the result of reform, not revolution. When they do occur, however, revolutions can broadly be differentiated on the basis of whether they are violent or non-violent, even though these ideal types can contain elements of the other. The 17th century Parliamentary revolution against King Charles I in England is illustrative of a violent revolution involving competing armies.

The Orange Revolution in Ukraine (2004-05), based on peaceful demonstrations (in part, rallied through text messaging), is an example of a non-violent revolution. A so-called cultural revolution is, in many respects, another variant of a non-violent revolution, being a bloodless paradigm shift in the way society defines and understands itself. The 18th century Enlightenment in Europe exemplifies a cultural revolution.

All revolutions entail massive transformations and involve complex turning points along the way. However, revolutionary activity is not a

normal part of a social pedagogue's work, even though inspiration might be taken from "revolutionary campaigners", such as King and Freire. The social pedagogic road to a more decent society relies on helping the oppressed, as did Freire, to unmask, critique and contest an unjust but taken-for-granted world. The task requires the deployment of local initiatives and social movements for social justice. In that role, social pedagogues can act as catalysts for collective efficacy beliefs by educating people about their rights and organising community action in defence of these entitlements. Communal buoyancy can then trigger civic activism, thereby enlarging what Unger (1987, p. 1) describes as 'our sense of the real and the possible' and fostering 'an openness to novelty' (ibid, p. 1). Such 'social plasticity' (ibid., p. 1) provides more flexibility and opportunism in a greatly widened sphere of democratic influence in both local and national politics.

In some cases (notably, when politicians refuse to repeal patently unjust laws), civil disobedience is a last resort. This implies taking non-violent political action contrary to law and in direct opposition to government policy. Simultaneously, civil disobedience invokes commonly held notions of fair play that are assumed to exist in society at large. It does this by standing up for:

> 'the sense of justice of the majority of the community and declares that in one's considered opinion the principles of social cooperation among free and equal men are not being respected (Rawls, 2003, p. 320).'

One of the boldest and most compassionate ways to practise civil disobedience is in solidarity with the oppressed. In his seminal essay, *Civil Disobedience* (1993), Harvard scholar, Henry David Thoreau (1817-1862), articulated this principle in forthright terms. He argued that in societies that imprison anyone unjustly, 'the true place for a just man is also a prison'. Thoreau's ideas were later to influence another great champion of civil rights, Martin Luther King. After reading Thoureau's essay, King concluded that it was right to side with good and wrong to side with evil. Based on this conviction, he developed a form of creative but non-violent protest against unjust laws. King's personal sacrifice was to embrace an idea whose time had come – equality for "people of colour" – and to pursue it as a supervening ethic that rose above unjust law even if this meant prison time. And he did go to prison for demonstrating against segregation in Birmingham Alabama. Ghandi, who also inspired King, was sent to prison several times too, mainly for opposing unprincipled British colonial politics in India.

KEY QUESTION

How would you respond to the assertion that civil disobedience in the cause of social justice is sometimes politically necessary and sometimes morally justifiable? Think of concrete examples that might illustrate your viewpoint.

In presenting my argument for compassionate practice in social pedagogy, I must concede a disclaimer of sorts. Even though I strongly believe that social pedagogy, as a normative discipline, should make compassion its cardinal virtue, I cannot *prove* that my conviction is right. I also think, but am unable to summon conclusive *proof,* that compassionate practice in social pedagogy serves social justice well. Yet for all that, in my heart – the most important part of a social pedagogue's anatomy – I *feel* that it is possible to adjudicate between different claims to right and wrong. Call this intuitive morality, but without felt conviction, anything goes. I really do think that most people believe in a fair chance for all in life. For example, I think most Britons would agree that poor people should have the same rights to health care as the rich. In that context, the UK National Health Service (NHS) is an example of politicised social justice, with clinical need rather than ability to pay being a core principle since its inception. It is worth taking a brief look at this important service.

Social justice in a welfare policy context

The launching of the NHS sprang from an explicit ethical goal: to take health care out of the fee-paying private market and to place it in the public service, where it would be free at the point of patient care. Before its inauguration in 1948, many people could not afford to see a doctor. In the 1930s, the British Medical Association (BMA) unveiled plans for general medical services for the entire nation. Many of the ideas in this blueprint were considered in the 1942 Beveridge Report, which looked at services that would be provided once the Second World War was over. Remarkably, given the overwhelming focus on the war effort, hospital surveys were conducted during the Second World War. The findings disclosed not only bed shortages and buildings in poor state of repair, but a lack of services in the most needy areas. Sir William Beveridge's report, *Social Insurance and Allied Services* (1942), proposed the setting up of a comprehensive healthcare service which would be free on the basis of clinical need. As a result, the National Health Service, as it was to be called (and still is) was founded in 1948 by the then Labour Minister of Health, Aneurin Bevan. Its ethic of needs-based as opposed to paid healthcare, has stood its ground for more than 60 years.

The NHS upholds the ethic of distributive justice by offering special attention to people in society who are relatively less healthy than the rest of the population. Furthermore, policymakers have stated that NHS staff must consult with patients and their carers (including family members) on all decisions about treatment. Being funded through national taxation, the NHS is answerable to the patients and communities it serves. This is not just about fiscal accountability but also concerns moral responsibility. One area in particular in the NHS, blood donation, epitomises the service's commitment to looking after the Other. The issue has been famously studied by the British social policy professor, Richard Titmuss (1997) in his book, *The Gift Relationship: From Human Blood to Social Policy*. The donation and distribution of blood in the NHS is based on voluntary giving, with no financial return. What this means, is that blood, a gift of life, is free to those who need it. The system leads to what Titmuss (1997, p. 59) sees as the fusing of 'the politics of welfare and the morality of individual wills'.

This idea of ethical reciprocity between politics and individual kindness exemplifies a truly compassionate social pedagogy, and evokes Natorp's (1904) vision of human solidarity. The principle also awakens Fourastié's (cited by Bauman, 2009, p. 61) idea of 'morales de peuple', by which he meant a morality from within. Such personal selflessness is a form of 'being for' (cf. Bauman, 2009, p. 61). Its institutional counterpart is found in a welfare state founded on social justice.

Concluding remarks

In concluding this chapter, it is appropriate to acknowledge social pedagogy's debt to one of its great founding fathers, Paul Natorp (1904). He set out a shaping value that guides compassionate social pedagogic practice: the putting aside of self-serving personal interest and the collective pursuit of everybody's interests. That is where the aspiration and the hope of social pedagogy is found today.

Chapter 5
Social pedagogic communication

'Out beyond ideas of right and wrong doing there is a field. I will meet you there.' (Jalaludin, 13ᵗʰ century Persian poet)

Introduction

In a formal sense, communication among people is, 'a form of human interaction conducted by means of signs and symbols' (International Commission for the Study of Communication Problems, 1978, p. 26).

KEY DEFINITION

Human communication defines human interaction that is conducted via signs and symbols.

Some linguists regard the words "signs" and "symbols" as working synonyms. Others think the words denote different meanings. There is, however, a compromise position. The words can be synonyms in some contexts, but not in others. For present purposes, and because I believe that signs and symbols are usually one and the same, I shall use "signs" to signify (i.e. stand for) both words. Signs take many forms, including, for example, words, tones of voice, gestures, images and artefacts. In human communication, words are arguably the most common signs. That said, a sign is a sign only if it is interpreted as a sign. Put simply, a sign must be understood to convey a meaning. If, for example, a social pedagogue says, "You are a very capable person", the listener must be able to recognise the positive content. It is also of interest to note that words can be interpreted in radically different ways.

Permit me to go back to the example of the Spanish word, "el señor" (see Chapter 4). El señor himself is likely to interpret this noun as "lord and master". In contrast, people of lower status who feel that el señor treats them unfairly probably take a different view. Perhaps the words, "el señor", signify the oppressor. Freire's (2007) work on how critical awareness can help the socially disadvantaged to discover the contempt in which they are held by the elite, is relevant here. If the oppressed remain within the el señor discourse, they will perceive themselves to be what the discourse permits, in this case, as inferior and under the authority of the master. To escape the discourse, a counter-discourse – for example, "I am a free human being" – must become the new representation of self. I return to the issue of discourse and counter-discourse later in the chapter. For now, though, I shall address the importance of communication in social pedagogic work.

KEY QUESTION

How easy or difficult do you think it might be for a socially disadvantaged human being to "learn" to reconceptualise social suffering as the result of oppression instead of a deserved or "natural" condition?

Communication in social pedagogic work

Communication is at the centre of social pedagogic practice. It is bound to be because social pedagogues are involved in caring relationships with other people. In broad terms, communication can occur as a discourse between equals or as a top-down, official discourse. Bernstein (1999) characterises the first ideal type as 'horizontal discourse' and the second as 'vertical discourse'. As a general rule, the interaction between the social pedagogue and the service user is based on horizontal communication. In this form of exchange the aim is to reach common understanding through reasoned discussion and cooperation. The practice suits social pedagogy well because it fosters user participation as opposed to professional monologue.

Nevertheless, the degree of service user involvement has to vary according to circumstances. Sometimes it will be overriding, at other times marginal. By way of illustration, let me consider "overriding" first. Over the past 40 years, the disability movement has played a key role in the "education" of the social professions to the extent that there has, at times, been a role reversal. When this has occurred, disabled people have shown the "experts" how social policy has failed to address the problem of barrier-creating environments. Such communicative power has been made possible not only through effective lobbying by disabled people, but also because they have engaged in dialogue with care professionals. There is an important lesson here. When service users have more say in decisions affecting *their* lives, self-motivation increases. In contrast, when "experts" make ultimatums, people do not necessarily feel bound to meet them (cf. Bandura, 1997).

KEY QUESTIONS
When is there scope in social pedagogic communication for a service user to
"teach" a care professional? From a social pedagogic perspective, would that be
a case of role reversal?

Notwithstanding, it would be wrong to think that vertical communication is always out of place. Communicative parity is an ideal rather than an edict. Yes, there is room for some discretionary freedom in the relationship between, for example, a child welfare pedagogue and a parent. But there are times when the professional has to take a decision that might place her in a potentially adversarial position vis-à-vis the other person. In cases, for example, involving egregious child abuse, she may need to place a child in care, even if a parent protests. Such decisions not only have a formal basis in law, but also represent expert knowledge in matters to which a professional rightly lays claim.

When social pedagogues need to be appropriately assertive, conveying the message respectfully is imperative. Moreover, through a process of helpful exchange, both parties can sometimes reach a solution that each can agree upon. The main thing is to avoid what Lewis (2003, p. 23) terms, 'doing-to, rather than doing-for or doing-with the client'.

So even when there are degrees of vertical affirmation in, for example, a child placement decision, there is also room for some horizontal communication. Thus, for example, a social pedagogue might consult a biological parent on his views concerning a particular placement.

Social pedagogues must also seek to ensure that their decisions are seen to be fair and reasonable and that expert knowledge is never privileged for its own sake. This requires a readiness to accept that a service user's standpoint might have credence despite a professional view to the contrary. That offers scope for reflective practice. The option is then open for the different parties to meet in the field that the 13th century Persian poet, Jalaludin (quoted at the head of this chapter), speaks of. Subsequently, if a social pedagogue concludes that a child's best interests can only be served by a decision that a parent opposes, avoiding a totalising and permanent stipulation may still be feasible. For example, if a child is placed in foster care, a discussion concerning expected duration and possible visits could encourage hope for the future.

It should also be emphasised that vertical communication does not necessarily imply that the different parties to a conversation are at odds with each other. Indeed, it is not uncommon for parents to consult a social pedagogue for advice on a family matter. Nor is it infrequent that a social pedagogue will educate a service user on his rights and how to secure them. Either way, a respectful and democratic exchange is the norm. There also needs to be a willingness on the part of the social pedagogue for the Other to be what she is, if that is her wish (cf. Rogers, 1997). The aim is to foster a "no blame" dialogue.

KEY QUESTION

Is it always possible in social pedagogic communication to maintain a "no blame" dialogue? Explain your answer.

In the ensuing encounter, social pedagogues are often able to do something that others are unable to do on their own (cf. Buber, 1997). This does not lead to inequality, but it does clarify respective roles; very important because ambiguity is unhelpful. The social pedagogue, as a professional, has a caring task to perform, and the "learner" is obliged to make an effort to enhance her own life chances. These are, as it were, the "rules of the game", but they are used in a communicative setting where emotional rapport is highly prized. This is why, in social pedagogic interaction, every effort is made to shorten the social distance between the helper and the recipient. Some service users feel labelled as in deficit as a result of encounters with bureaucrats who regard personal problems as personal failures. Sure, there might be things that a service user could have done better. However, the issue is not to judge but to enable and support perceived self-efficacy.

Once a positive emotional connectedness is established, this positions the social pedagogue as a caring partner rather than an aloof expert. Moreover, the rational advice that is proffered is couched in a warm communication style that is genuine and compassionate. This creates, if you will allow the cliché, a "win, win" situation: a confluence of reason and humanity in the service of the Other. While the instrumental part of the encounter (planned goals, etc.) is crucial to the outcome, the social pedagogue in me still cherishes the affective joy of seeing a broken human being rising to the challenge of a once "insuperable" problem and discovering that it was not unbeatable after all.

Rosenberg (no date; no pagination) also underscores the importance of affect in compassionate communication. He (2003) believes that heartfelt exchange is the precursor of heartfelt generosity. The giver of comfort gladly bestows this gift and, knowing this is so, the recipient accepts it without feeling burdensome. If emotional rapport is absent in social pedagogic relationships, communication is dry and lacks gusto. To avoid a perfunctory conversation, the social pedagogue needs to establish a warm and kindly tone from the outset. This can be accomplished through a reassuring style that involves, for example, friendliness, nodding, smiling, paraphrasing and encouraging. The aim is to put the service user at ease before dealing with the practicalities.

That is not to diminish the importance of the instrumental aspects of the social pedagogue's work. Rather, it is about the recognition of priorities, namely, when to summon the heart and when to apply the head.

KEY TASK

Illustrate with a real or imagined example, how instrumental and compassionate communication can complement each other in social pedagogic communication.

The heart and the head parts

As should be clear by now, I regard social pedagogic work as moral work. It started with a moral purpose (Natorp, 1904) and despite some ugly deviations along the road (notably, the misuse of the discipline during Hitler's Third Reich), its moral compass is largely intact in Continental Europe today. There will, unquestionably, be some examples of "social pedagogic malpractice", but these are surely the exception rather than the rule. In its contemporary context, then, social pedagogic work is, by and large, stirred by the heart and is wary of officialdom, particularly when red tape compromises social justice. At the same time, the head, in the right place and at the right time, is indispensable. Once the heart has shown its kindly disposition, the head is ready to deliberate and to do so in the best interests of the Other. There is, in short, a necessary synchronization here between expressive communication (the heart) and instrumental communication (the head). The heart feels and the head knows what needs to be done. And *forever* the twain shall meet, provided they are not on a collision course!

The point is that communication can be more than just an exchange of information. People swap emotions too. For example, Subject A provides information to Subject B, who feels insulted and communicates her anger. What happens next is anybody's guess. Perhaps, Subject A replies in a conciliatory tone, perhaps not. She might simply respond in a matter-of-fact way: "Those are the rules and you must follow them". Interestingly, social constructionists note how emotional communication often relies (with the possible exception of uncharacteristic outbursts) on culturally prescribed "emotional rules" (cf. Bartsch, 2004).

This suggests that an individual who self-ascribes an emotional form of communication at will, might find herself out of the step with the conventional script, and consequently pay the price. That said, there may be scope for a symbolic negotiation of emotions (Bartsch, 2004). In that regard, it is necessary to understand that what constitutes socially approved behavior is often context-specific. This implies that those unversed with the "script" might unknowingly break the rules. Let me illustrate the point and the hypothetical consequences with an imaginary example.

An unemployed man from a Mediterranean country, where family often look after their own (including the elderly sick), comes to Norway in search of work. There, in contrast, it is quite common for institutions to take a more conspicuous role in the care of sick older people. The job-seeker visits a Norwegian employment office. A member of staff suggests that he might wish to consider a post as a care assistant in a local care home for older people. So far, information has been communicated in an instrumental fashion. However, the idea that the job-seeker might want to work in this institution, prompts an emotionally charged response: "I could never work in that place. It would be tantamount to helping families to ignore their responsibilities."

As in my other imagined scenario, it would be speculative to second-guess what might occur next. However, from a social pedagogic perspective, it would be polite and professional to respond in a respectful manner. Accordingly, listening carefully and empathically, helps one to understand the other's viewpoint; and showing tolerance of difference (provided the other opinion is not patently unreasonable), shows forbearance. It is also helpful, and here I invoke a Habermasian approach, to work hard to try to reach a decision that both parties can agree to. I shall say more about Habermas later in the chapter. Meanwhile, during the search for consensus – and this actually touches upon Bartsch's (2004) point about negotiating emotions – each party should allow the other to show their feelings, and do so with consideration and courtesy.

In a somewhat different setting, but still on the theme of emotional and instrumental exchange, Bensing and Dronkers (1992) distinguish between two types of communication during doctor-patient interactions:

1. Affective communication: creating a therapeutic relationship as the basis for gaining the patient's confidence and for being able to handle the pyscho-social climate.

2. Instrumental communication: necessary information exchange for dealing with specific problems.

Applied to the social pedagogic relationship, these forms of communication can be illustrated in the following way. A lone mother with a 9-year-old son has a meeting with a social pedagogue. The mother is a wheelchair user and finds it hard to engage in social activities with the boy, such as watching him play football, going to the cinema with him and having a holiday together. Even though her son knows it is not his mum's fault, he is upset that she is unable to do these things.

The first priority of the social pedagogue in cases like this is to listen attentively and with genuine sympathy. This is the heart part. Her attention is on relationship building with the service user. Once the person feels emotionally comfortable and secure, the next step, through dialogue, is to find solutions. In the above example, this will probably involve a combination of by-proxy and efficacy promoting approaches. The by-proxy part might, for example, involve the provision of personal assistance if that is agreeable to the service user. Many countries now provide personal assistants to wheelchair users in the form of a personalised service that is largely decided by the disabled person. Explaining what the service entails requires an instrumental conversation with attention to practical issues. This is the head part. Notwithstanding, instrumentality is in the service of a compassionate aim, namely, to provide necessary care in an efficient manner.

As regards efficacy building, even though this also involves some instrumental aspects (e.g. concrete task setting), emotional support is crucial. Helping people to believe in their innate and potential capacities requires encouragement, reassurance and praise. In addition, it is better to focus on past successes rather than dwell on previous failures. Lifting the spirit is an important goal in social pedagogic work. A despondent mood weakens motivation, whereas a positive mood elevates a sense of personal efficacy (Bandura, 1997). Again in the example referred to, the social pedagogue might reassure the wheelchair user that personal support would allow her, as a mother, to play a greater role in her son's life outside the home, which is what her son wants. It would also be appropriate to point out that the son's wish shows his strong attachment to a good mum.

Quite often, people come to a social pedagogue in a state of emotional distress. That is not surprising given that many socially disadvantaged people 'have borne the brunt of a misinformed, callous, social policy' (Lewis, 2003, p. 24). What they need is kindness and comfort offered in a heartfelt way. With this in mind, the work of the American psychologist, Carl Rogers (Rogers et al, 1967; see also Rogers, 1958), on the helping relationship is particularly salient. If helpful change is to be achieved, the therapist must be able to present herself as a person who:

- Is genuine and is recognised by her client as being so.

- Shows a positive regard for her client.

- Demonstrates an empathic understanding of her client's world.

Rogers (1958; 1967)

An emotionally secure setting is the basis of all helping relationships; or should be.

KEY QUESTION

Do you agree that an emotionally secure setting must be the basis of any helping relationship? Give reasons.

This applies just as much in social pedagogic work as it does in psychotherapy. The aim in both cases is to communicate that the person is not being blamed. On the contrary, the social pedagogue feels for the Other's predicament. This warm empathy helps to build a climate of trust. On the practical level, there is of course work to be done, but the social pedagogue is there to comfort as well as to set tasks. Horizontal communication calls upon the heart and the head. It signals intense personalism and clarity in context-appropriate doses. This necessary balance is fundamental because social pedagogues often face a painful choice. They work in institutions that are supposed to care but whose antiseptic protocols stifle "too much" gentleness. It is hard to be openly passionate in such settings.

KEY QUESTIONS

Is it possible for care professionals to "learn" how to communicate in an appropriate emotional way in social pedagogic settings? If so, how? If not, why not?

I am reminded of the American abolitionist, William Lloyd Garrison (1805-1879) who not only sought the immediate emancipation of slaves but also spoke in favour of the women's suffrage movement. Garrison was once asked why he was 'all on fire'. He replied: 'I have need to be all on fire, for I have mountains of ice about me to melt' (cited by Kozol, 1993, p. 18). In some ways, Garrison's moral outrage is surely felt by social pedagogues who feel constrained to act in an emancipatory way by institutional regimes that set limits to human kindness. My reply is that the first responsibility of the social pedagogue is to the service user, not the service institution or the state. If, however, institutions legitimate their power in the form of socially just authority and are genuinely responsive to the needs of the oppressed, then there is no moral quandary (cf. Herrmann, 2005).

There is, though, another problem. As servants of the state, some welfare managers are more inclined to hold individuals to account than society. If that discourse is firmly entrenched, achieving a more enlightened way of seeing is a gruelling undertaking.

KEY QUESTION

Is emotional connectedness between a care professional and a service user necessary, or is there the risk that this might jeopardise professional judgement?

Discourse and counter-discourse

Dominant discourses generally announce themselves as exclusive and complete, even timeless; and certainly not open to scrutiny. This has attracted much criticism, not least from egalitarian academics. For example, in his analysis of human sexuality, Foucault (1990) refuses to

115

treat sexuality as a historically singular concept. On the contrary, social notions of approved sexuality are heavily context-bound. This can be seen, for instance, in attitudes towards homosexuality. Engaging in homosexual acts carries the death penalty in some countries, yet gay marriages are allowed in other countries.

Foucault's (1990) point is that the social constructions of the powerful in society, *their discourses*, have major consequences with regard to legitimacy issues. Let me refer to a parallel in another dominant discourse, the notion of "undeserving welfare recipients". This stigmatising label is often attached to people who receive benefits, even when they are morally and legally within their full rights to do so. It conveys an indignant (even angry) view of lazy people, living off the state. Furthermore, it is part of a neo-liberal discourse that prizes personal independence in a society that is said not to exist. There are only individuals, said Mrs Thatcher, implying that this is how it should be. That pitiless fable is, tragically, still with us. The trouble with half-baked and hurtful discourses is that they not only hang around in the air but also enter social exchanges, including those that occur in social welfare offices. At this point, negative labels can, 'act like shrieking sirens, deafening us to all finer discriminations that we might otherwise perceive' (Allport, 1979, p. 179). Allport was referring specifically to racist stereotypes, but the same process generally applies to any group that is labelled as deviant.

Social pedagogues in societies where neo-liberal politics prevail are at risk, perhaps unwittingly, of regarding paid employment or earned pension as the only legitimate forms of income. If they hold this view, they are likely to take a dim view of vulnerable groups such as the unemployed. On the other hand, social pedagogues who have a more critical outlook go against the proverbial grain by being radical. This phenomenon is more common than expected. In the US, for example, which has a minimal welfare state, there is a long and noble tradition of radical (the left-wing kind) social work.

KEY TASK

Based on your knowledge of the society in which you live, how common do you think negative discourses about social welfare recipients seem to be? Feel free to refer to personal impressions and/or empirical evidence. As appropriate, refer to illustrative examples.

116

Professionals and scholars in the social work profession have promoted the cause of social justice, and have done so despite longstanding distrust of social welfare in governing circles. There is, so to speak, a "disconnect" between the discourse of those who stand by the socially disadvantaged and the unsympathetic politics of Capitol Hill. In the Nordic countries, by contrast, there is more (but not complete) accord between the radical professional perspective and the government position. This is largely because Nordic welfare is, in many respects, "normalised" rather than stigmatised. My point here is that the receipt of social revenues is seen as customary and universal, and therefore not something to be unduly embarrassed about.

Indeed, pre-service socialisation into radical social pedagogic roles is the norm in countries such as Norway (Stephens, 2011b). This makes it less likely that social pedagogues and politicians will be at odds with each other because, by and large, both regard welfare as a necessary and civilised response to the vagaries of the life span. If though, for whatever reason, an oppressive discourse defines and dominates welfare politics, it must be confronted robustly and consistently. The key instrument here is an emancipatory counter-discourse heavily reliant on participatory forms of communication. The two adverbs, "robustly" and "consistently", signal that the participatory aspect is hardy and unswerving. There is a lot of impression management and paper-dressing in the political rhetoric surrounding user participation. As Arnstein (1969) convincingly points out, there is a big difference between going through empty motions and actually having the wherewithal to affect decision-making. With this in mind, it is necessary to be wary of phoney rhetoric.

Participatory communication: barriers and potentials

At the risk of pushing my point beyond empirical verification, I think the main barrier to participatory communication (which is usually horizontal), is authoritarianism. People who like to tell other people what to do in no-nonsense terms, also favour hierarchies and especially command structures that give them lots of power, but rarely should I add much authority. Such despotism reveals a deep distrust for others, especially with regard to those deemed unable to take responsibility for their own affairs. The oppressed, poor and socially disadvantaged (statuses that typically co-exist) are the usual suspects. Unfortunately, it is easy to fall into the trap (with varying levels of culpability) of becoming an authoritarian communicator when working with people who encounter a lot of hardship in life. The temptation is to judge, blame, decide on a "remedy" and dispatch. If this habitus becomes ingrained, not only does it work against the best interests of the service user, it becomes hard to dislodge. Consider, for example, the problems that are bound to arise if social workers, nurses, disability therapists and child welfare pedagogues are distrustful of their "clients", seeing them as calculating opportunists.

Such welfare professionals, though I suspect few in number, do exist. And what do they have in common? They lack a basic understanding of human relations and are quick to stigmatise those less fortunate, such as attributing to the poor, 'an objectionable .... *well-deserved reputation*' (Zawadski,1948, cited by Allport, 1979, p. 87). I should add that the reference to 'well-deserved' is Zawadski's documentation, not his approval, of prejudice. Regardless of professional background, "blame game" communicators often use the following techniques (cf. Freire, 2007):

- Mechanical transfer: the uncritical allocation of "expert" knowledge to "non-experts" and the depositing of this in presumed unthinking objects, not thinking subjects.

- Cultural invasion: adopting a conquest mind set in which an "expert's" doxa (taken-for granted view of the world) is imposed on a "non-expert".

- Dictating: a particularly aggressive form of cultural invasion, whereby the authoritarian person seeks to force his ideology on others.

- Manipulation: a covert and shrewd form of communication in which one who offers seemingly benevolent advice has ulterior motives.

These techniques can promote docility and passive acceptance.

KEY TASK

Select one of the above communication techniques, and demonstrate how, in a practice situation (real or imagined), it might promote docility and passive acceptance.

Another barrier to participatory communication is present in what Swartz (2007) terms an 'individualist discourse'. In that perspective, the oppressed are seen to have themselves to blame. Furthermore, structural factors beyond personal control are played down. Individuals do, of course, have to assume a level of responsibility, but this must be proportionate. How absurd it would be, for example, to expect a lone, unemployed parent to seek employment if child care is unavailable or too costly. Individualist discourse conveys the privileged habitus of the self-styled expert. She speaks; others listen. Hers is thus a vertical conversation derived from institutional authority. Foucault (1972, p. 217) identifies this type of communication in the analysis of a meeting between a doctor and 'a madman'. Even today, he notes (ibid, p. 217), 'this procedure still takes place in the context of a hiatus between listener and speaker'.

In the worst situations, as Lipsky (1980) documents, health and care workers refer to some service users as 'deadbeats', 'garbage', 'scum', 'liars' and so forth. Such forms of symbolic violence reflect the superiority that certain functionaries think they have over working class people and the contempt reserved for "dissidents" and other "troublemakers". But there is hope and it lies in critical awareness. Derisory stereotypes of welfare recipients, even the well-concealed ones, can be identified and assiduously avoided. Of particular importance, social pedagogues and other professions must strive to keep their attitudes in touch with first-hand experience.

Witnessing oppressed individuals bravely struggling to care for their families under extreme duress – not of their own making, I should add – is a powerful corrective to prejudice in such harrowing circumstances. Not only does frontline work help social pedagogues to confront destructive discourse, it also fosters a counter-discourse firmly grounded in humane values and reliable professional knowledge. The good news is that honest counter-discourse is contagious. It passes from social pedagogue to service user in the sense that the former's perspective helps the latter to challenge the negative stereotypes that oppressed people often have of themselves. There are strong pedagogic echoes here of Freire's (2007) work with the disenchanted poor of Brazil. Just as they can, so can the poor and oppressed of Europe stop clinging to unsustainable, indeed patently false, images of their own "powerlessness".

That requires a re-writing of their own sense of who they are and, crucially, what they are really worth and are able to achieve. The new affirmation, pedagogically tutored and then tested in the real word, is couched in positive rather than defeatist language: "I am a human being with worth who has the capacity to change things for the better." There is nothing "touchy, feely" about this. In the spirit of Allport (1979), there is instead the self-assured belief that the rational and moral potential of human beings are powerful correctives to self-destructive despair and resignation. Yes, the task ahead might look foreboding, especially for those of the poor who have been relentlessly dubbed as welfare scroungers by politicians and in the tabloid media. It is a daunting task to contest this carefully orchestrated barrage of negative imagery. The problem is compounded if people have habituated a low self-image over a long period. Helping service users to see themselves in a positive light is therefore an essential goal in social pedagogic communication.

For this reason, the social pedagogue has an obligation to frame her language in a manner that envisages the service user as a potential change agent who has nothing to be ashamed of and much to be proud of. It is also important to engage in gentle, respectful dialogue, thereby opening a space for non-judgemental reflection. In this space, the social pedagogue and the Other can free themselves of fatalistic determinism so that they can discover together the power of change agency. That is the social pedagogic challenge of communicative virtuosity: to help self-doubting people up to the brink of what Piaget (in Bringuier, 1990) terms, a process of accommodation, namely, to learn by seeing things in a different light. The desired outcome of social pedagogic learning is a positive change in self-representation.

Yet even when a service user refuses to believe that her social world can be re-defined, the onus is on the social pedagogue to persevere and to do so with dignity. This evokes Habermas's (2005, p. 55) argument that:

> 'Even in cases of conflict, the persons involved are to go on interacting in an attitude of communicative action. They are to attune themselves, from the participant perspective of a first person, to the other as a second person, with the intention of reaching an understanding with him instead of reifying and instrumentalizing him, in the observer perspective of a third person, for their own ends'.

In the communicative setting described by Habermas (2005), it is the social pedagogue's responsibility to take the moral initiative of keeping the conversation going and not losing sight of the other person's standpoint. The hope is that a consensus will eventually arise. It probably will, but if it does not, all is not lost. For, even when discussants are poles apart in their views, empathic understanding can result in greater

120

awareness of the issues and reasons that prevent agreement (Weber, 1949). As indicated above, participatory communication owes much of its legacy to Freire (1996a), who is famous for his pioneering pedagogic work with the poor in North-Eastern Brazil. Central in Freire's approach was helping the oppressed to identify and pursue *their* role in *their* future rather than having these mapped out by outside "experts" or the self-interested rich. This radical self-scrutiny sits uneasily with pernicious forms of vertical discourse, and fosters horizontal communication based on equal respect for both parties.

KEY QUESTION

Do expert knowledge and opinion ever have a role to play in social pedagogic dialogue? Explain your answer.

It is important to note that Freire's commitment to horizontal communication does not imply that two parties to a conversation necessarily have the same roles. In his work on student-teacher relationships, Freire made it clear that students and teachers are different. But, adds Freire (1996b, p. 162), 'if the teacher has opted for democracy, he or she cannot allow this difference to become antagonistic'. In other words, different does not denote inferior or superior. It simply describes distinct roles. Moreover the same democratic principles still apply: distinct roles; same humanity. Initial face-to-face meetings between social pedagogues and service users often start with an arranged appointment. At this time, it is helpful to give service users maximum opportunity to talk about how they want to change their futures for the better. After all, social pedagogy is about self-efficacious change agency. Communication is open and honest and ideas can be formulated, re-considered and re-formulated as the conversation proceeds.

There are no pre-ordained decisions, but rather a joint quest for the best answers and a better future. This entails horizontal participation in an exchange of ideas between the two persons, both of them as subjects. Such an approach is in stark contrast to a "sender-receiver" conversation, in which the professional does most of the talking and the service user does most of the listening. That kind of vertical communication turns service users into objects of expert knowledge rather than equal partners. It should therefore be avoided.

The ideal communicative model in social pedagogy is described by Jackson (2006, p. 69) as 'mutuality', which he aptly defines, 'as the respectful give-and-take between and among persons'. Mutuality embraces the principle of a coming together between the social pedagogue and the service user in a spirit of friendship, which is to be distinguished from friendliness. The latter can sometimes takes the shape of superficial outgoingness; the former is perhaps more likely to be based on authentic trust. Another interesting idea that social pedagogues can helpfully borrow from is found in Habermas's (1999, p. 4) argument that:

> '[M]oral obligations recommend themselves by their internal relation to the gentle, persuasive force of reasons as an alternative to strategic, that is, coercive or manipulative, forms of conflict resolution.'

Should discord arise between a social pedagogue and a service user, it is wise not to "pull rank", if that can be avoided. Instead, every effort should be made to listen politely and to respond with empathy. This is especially important when dealing with family problems. Parents can become very possessive about matters concerning their children. Rather than pushing them into a corner, a better approach is to offer them reasonable choices. By exploring options together and being open to the idea that a third alternative might exist, a joint resolution is more likely to be achieved.

At the same time, I must reiterate that it is desirable, in so far as this is possible, to reach a common understanding that both parties can by and large morally agree upon. Habermas's (1979) work is especially cogent in this regard. For him, speaking to another person with the aim of reaching a common understanding must involve a moral dimension:

> 'The speaker must want to express his intentions truthfully [*wahrhaftig*] so that the hearer can believe the utterance of the speaker (can trust him)' (Habermas, 1979, pp. 2-3).

Habermas (1979) adds that the communicative task of coming to an accord is not just about understanding what words mean. It also concerns agreeing on the moral rightness that the words express. In the case of social pedagogic practice, this will involve the recognition that the service user's use of language might be different to that of the social pedagogue. That requires sensitivity to dialects and other non-standard forms of English. Some people express indignation by cussing, others by raising their voices and yet others through tears or angry outbursts. Each type of articulation calls for considerate interpretation rather than hasty defensive reactions. The same principle applies to body language, which can signal a whole variety of emotional states. And, yes, in stressful circumstances, some service users will have a short fuse. When things get heated, it is unwise to try to prove the other person wrong.

It is preferable, whenever feasible, to seek a common resolution. In keeping with respect for the Other, a sensible social pedagogic response would be to hear the person out and to remain as calm as possible. This does not compromise professional assertiveness, but it does let the heated service user vent her feelings. Often, the most respectful kind of democratic communication is found in what Habermas (2005, p. 56) describes as, 'the "we"-perspective from which we perceive one another as members of an *inclusive* community no person is excluded from'. Habermas (1999) also goes to great lengths in his defence of non-coercive interaction. This is a reliable guarantor of civilised debate and conveys the Kantian imperative of respect for the Other. Buber's (2004) notion of the I-Thou relationship, which he contrasts with the I-It counterpart, fits in well here because the I shows its whole self and also meets the Thou as another whole person.

In an atmosphere of mutual trust, the parties to a conversation can be honest about their 'relatively autonomous "vested knowledges" ' (Foucault, 1994, pp. 6-7). Once made explicit, different opinions can then be subjected to joint (but never cynical) scrutiny. This mode of communication prevents professional monologues from taking over the conversation (cf. Foucault, 2008, p. 24). That does not imply a rejection of established truths out of hand. Rather, the intention is to invite participatory investigation, and, if needs be, to disturb what Foucault (2008, p. 28) refers to as, 'the tranquillity with which they (established truths) are accepted'. Claims to totalising knowledge (Habermas, 1984) are best kept out of dialogic communication because they diminish the relevance of context-sensitivity. For example, a welfare-to-work approach might help some unemployed people, but, depending on circumstances, there are also other options to be considered.

KEY TASK

Assess the argument that the goal of arriving at common accord in social pedagogic relationships poses the risk that one or more parties to a conversation might simply "cave in "and agree just to keep the peace.

Societies differ in their receptiveness to participatory communication. In the US, for example, where a Strict Father discourse is strong in welfare settings (Lakoff, 2002), vertical communication is prized. The objective is to get the service user to obey, and self-reliance is the command. "Go out and get a job" (even if this means, as it usually does, a low paid job), is the politician's solution to poverty. In Norway, by contrast, where a Nurturant Parent model (cf. Lakoff, 2002) is more to the fore, social pedagogues understand the importance and the justice of finding structural remedies to structural problems. Illustrative of this approach (but in another country), Pugh and Richards (1996) report on the implementation of a practical intervention involving mental health service users across a large rural county in the UK. Their study showed how a group of service users who were often isolated could speak out and be heard. Through group work sessions, service users discussed their experiences of the services they had received. Subsequently, they presented their views to County and local joint planning teams. This community pedagogy led to several improvements in service provision.

Concluding remarks

On that optimistic note, it is pertinent that the study by Pugh and Richards (1996), reawakens Natorp's (1904) social pedagogic ideal of a society where individual wilfulness is put to collective purpose, so that all may benefit. There are many pre-conditions for this achievable utopia, among them, respectful and dialogic communication in social pedagogic practice.

Chapter 6
Cross-national lesson-drawing

'A Nation, like a person, has a mind – a mind that must be kept informed and alert, that must know itself, that understands the hopes and the needs of its neighbors – all the other Nations that live within the narrowing circle of the world' (Franklin D. Roosevelt, 1941)

Introduction

A few years ago, a Los Angeles mother became the first person on the American West Coast to donate a kidney. The surgeon used a pioneering procedure. This made it easier for the donor to give the gift of life to the recipient by reducing recovery time and post-operative pain. The operation, single-port donor nephrectomy, now makes it possible for a donor to be out of hospital in two or three days and back to normal routines within two weeks. Although the surgery was performed in the US, medical craft skills transfer well outside a nation's borders.

This is because surgical procedures that are based on Western medicine contain general principles which can be applied in any national setting. In contrast, social pedagogy is a markedly context-sensitive discipline. Thus, for example, social pedagogic practices can and do vary – at least, to some extent – in different national settings. To illustrate the point, cuddling an anxious child in a pre-school might be considered appropriate in some nations but not in others. These and other variations often hinge on distinct political traditions. Take healthcare, for example. In the US, President Obama signed the Affordable Care Act into law in 2010. This was a brave but risky action. American conservatives (those with a big "C" and a little "c") are wary of the Act because, for them, it smacks of "European Socialism". This is why ObamaCare is having a bumpy ride.

Republicans, in particular, tend to see public healthcare as a form of mollycoddling that goes against the grain of self-reliance. So embedded is this value in American culture, that even US military veterans, the revered heroes of political ceremony, often get a raw deal when they return home. In fact, one third of them are homeless and hungry in the US today (The Veterans Site, 2012).

In this chapter, I examine the potential for cross-national learning in the field of social pedagogy, focusing mainly on what the UK might discover from Continental Europe and even implement. I say "implement", but it is more precise to speak of adoption and adaptation. Lock, stock and barrel copying from abroad is rarely a wise choice, especially when a social science is under consideration. With regard to welfare policy, Continental Europe (and, especially, the Nordic countries) and the UK already share some basic characteristics, so prudent cross-national learning does seem viable. Both geographical areas have found, in varying degrees, a middle path between erstwhile Soviet Communism and contemporary (but softened) neo-liberalism. The upshot is state regulated, socially mediated capitalism and welfare systems that serve entire populations.

The nature of cross-national lesson-drawing

Any proposal concerning cross-national lesson -drawing must address a fundamental question, and it is this. Is it possible that ideas and practices in one national setting could be applied in a different national setting? A lot of researchers are addressing this issue, and the literature contains an array of colourful descriptors: 'lesson-drawing'; 'policy borrowing'; 'policy shopping'; and 'policy band-wagoning', to name but some (Stone, 2000).

I think that 'lesson-drawing' is a helpful concept. Not only is it erudite and sharp, it also invites reflective contemplation. There is a sense in which lesson-drawing opens up the possibility of wheedling out aspects of promising practice elsewhere rather than the whole package. I use the word, "possibility", advisedly. In some cases, for example, it might actually be wise to import a compendium rather than an over-diluted version.

I would like to illustrate this point. In earlier chapters, I have referred to an anti-school bullying programme that some schools have adopted in Norway: the Olweus programme. This particular intervention has a long and distinguished pedigree. Indeed, the positive effects of the measure – notably, substantial reductions (up to 50% or more) in students' reports of bullying and victimization – have been verified in numerous scientific studies over the past two decades; not just in Norway, but also in replication programmes in, for example, England, the US and Iceland (cf. Center for the Study and Prevention of Violence [CSPV], 2007; Norwegian Ministry of Education and Norwegian Ministry of Children & Families, 2000; Limber et al, 2004; The Olweus Group, 2004).

The message here is that the full potential of the Olweus Programme can only be achieved if teachers trust and implement it pretty much intact. To do otherwise, would be to import a different anti-school bullying programme. Against this opinion, it could be argued that some schools prefer to adopt ideas which permit a degree of "in-house" adaptation. Ultimately, I suppose the final decision must be based on the degree of fidelity to the original that an adopting country chooses to make. There is, of course, a middle way. An importer nation could incorporate the core components of a social pedagogic programme and then make small adjustments, as deemed appropriate to local conditions.

Back to 'lesson-drawing'. This is, in fact, the term that Professor Richard Rose (2001), a leading scholar in the field of cross-national learning, has chosen to use. So I am in good company. Rose is mindful that lessons must not be drawn via naïve imitation, but by gathering edifying information from a programme in operation. This strikes me as a middle-ground position between lock, stock and barrel and arbitrary cherry-picking.

Although local context is always important, problems with adjustment are not necessarily insurmountable. So-called transfer agents, whether these are politicians, civil servants, academics or a community of interest acting in concert, must be open to the possibility that what is done well there might also be done well here. Healthy scepticism is obviously appropriate, so in order to safeguard rational inquiry and avoid rash conjecture, Rose (2001) has proposed a helpful checklist of necessary steps when appraising models elsewhere. These apply to cross-national lesson-drawing in general, not to social pedagogic measures in particular:

Step 1. Diagnose the home problem. For example, it might be found that increasing the access of disabled people to professions such as nursing, social work, medicine and teaching, needs more input from disabled people themselves. This conclusion could lead to an examination of good inclusive practice in other countries.

Step 2. Decide where to look for a potentially promising lesson. Lots of countries offer evidence of good practice. However, it can be prudent to narrow the field to countries that have the following characteristics: similar values and psychological mind-sets to the home country; proportionate resources for implementation; available and easily accessible evidence (e.g. summaries in English); interdependence, as, for example, in EU funding of cross-national feasibility projects.

Step 3. Investigate how a programme works abroad. This requires on-site evaluation in order to find out how the intervention functions from the inside and how it is viewed in the exporter country. In that endeavour, the opinions of the "foot-soldiers" who provide the service are just as important as the perspectives of those who design it. Soliciting the views of academics who know the programme well is sensible too. This is not to forget the experiences of the real experts, namely, the recipients of a particular service. Finally, it is wise to consider the standpoint of programme critics, thereby providing a degree of balance.

Step 4. Distil a cause-and-effect model for export. This kind of abstraction necessitates concentrating on main features. The basic elements can then be simulated in settings that are adapted to local conditions and re-tooled in accordance with contextual exigencies. A lesson-drawing model should abide by the principle of Occam's razor, omitting all non-essentials and focusing on everything necessary to make the programme work.

Step 5. Design a lesson. The adaption of the exported model to the circumstances of the imported setting is a key challenge when designing a lesson. The closer the correspondence between the design of the model in its country of origin and the envisaged operation in its new circumstances, the easier it will be to compare empirical effects. However, this does not rule out the possibility of hybrid design of the kind, for example, that combines compatible elements of programmes from several countries.

Step 6. Decide whether to import. As a general principle, policymakers will only support lesson-drawing if it is congenial to their opinions regarding what governments ought and ought not to do. For example, policymakers who believe that government should provide universal welfare are more inclined to listen and learn from overseas governments that support national health policies.

Step 7. Handle resource needs and restraints. Programme costs and available resources are critical in this regard. Can a poor country afford to implement a costly programme from a rich country? How can the UK emulate social pedagogic practice from Continental Europe when only a few British universities offer degrees in social pedagogy? These are important considerations. That said, it is wise to consider the maxim, "Never say never" because circumstances change, and sometimes rapidly. Take Norway, for example. Prior to oil and gas discoveries in the 1960s, it was not a rich country. Yet today, the United Nations regards it as the richest nation on earth.

Step 8. Take due account of contextual challenges. In any one nation, existing policy arrangements typically consist of a matrix of established programmes. Given that a programme needs to be anchored within the political and cultural institutions of government, a lesson cannot be imported if there are no compatible institutions in the home country that can realistically implement it.

Step 9: Conduct prospective evaluation. This step is at least as important as assessing things after implementation. For that reason, prospective evaluation is vital if policymakers can decide whether or not a programme there shows potential here. This practice is commonly used in fiscal policy. When a modification is proposed to an existing tax, the future effects of the change on public revenue are estimated based on what has happened in the past. In this sense, looking ahead functions as a form of "accident prevention", providing warnings of possible perils.

Step 10. Use overseas countries as "positive" or "negative" models. If a programme is borrowed from a country that is held in high international esteem, this can enhance the attractiveness of the lesson independently of its potential merit. The converse is also true. There is, of course, the risk of placing too much emphasis on perceptions of country profiles. A good model can conceivably be found anywhere.

Rose's (2001) "checklist" is a sober warning not to be duped by the "Grass is greener ..." adage. It is not exhaustive though, so there will be risks. The point is to be brave but not reckless. Essentially, there is a policy transfer continuum varying from obvious non-starters to promising prospects. With that thought in mind, it is time to consider the exportability potential of social pedagogy. I shall focus on exportability to the home nation, in this particular case, the UK.

Is social pedagogy exportable to the UK?

There is no easy answer to the question posed. But that has not stopped foremost researchers at the University of London from trying to arrive at an informed opinion. This endeavour has been made easier by a readiness on the part of UK policymakers to draw ideas from social pedagogic theory and practice abroad (Petrie et al, 2006). Evidence for this is found in a number of policy documents. For example, *Every Child Matters* (DfES, 2003) and *The Children's Plan* (DCSF, 2007) contain policy ambitions for uniting care and education services as children's services in all local authorities. This recalls a hallmark feature of social pedagogic practice, namely, keeping affective and cognitive processes close to the chest. More recently, the *2020 Children and Young People's Workforce Strategy* (DCSF 2008) committed the government to developing a Youth Professional Status for care professionals based on a social pedagogic model.

This and other government documents on the child workforce indicate that the profession of social pedagogue has finally reached UK shores and that it represents a role that should be imported and selectively imitated (cf. Cameron et al, 2010). It is also heartening to find that the British government recently funded the implementation of a Continental European model of social pedagogic practice in an English setting. That entailed the employment of 42 overseas-educated social pedagogues (mainly from Germany) in 18 English children's homes. Supported by a team of academics from the Thomas Coram Research Unit and funded by the now Department for Education from 2009 to 2011, the "experiment" was intended to make some social pedagogic 'ripples' in English residential childcare (Cameron et al, 2011). And it succeeded.

Independent evaluation of the project (Berridge et al, 2011) found that most managers and heads of homes, as well as the social pedagogues themselves, believed that residential practice had gained from overseas social pedagogic expertise. The intervention was well adapted to local and agency policies and it was thought that standards of care had improved. Reassuringly, British residential staff admired the high status of the social pedagogues, and also their professionalism. Moreover, a social pedagogic approach seemed to reduce anomic tendencies in residential homes. On the other hand, Berridge et al (2011) noted that some aspects of social pedagogy were at odds with English values. For example, the egalitarian nature of the discipline, with its emphasis on democratic relations between care providers and young people, was less well received. Give it time, is my advice! British society needs time to relinquish the unhelpful aspects of hierarchy and social control in its care and educational institutions.

The pilot study referred to above is of special interest because it has accomplished a goal that Petrie and Cameron (2009, p. 145) set a few years ago: ' "trying it [social pedagogy] on for size" '. Interestingly, Essex County Council (Boyce, 2010) tried it on for size too. In December 2008, the Council introduced social pedagogy to all 12 of its children's homes. Two years on, 157 staff had undertaken an introductory six-day course in the subject, which at that time represented more than a third of the county's children's residential workforce. The overwhelming majority of the participants expressed satisfaction with the trial, which had sparked numerous examples of positive practice in the homes. These included more creative activities with young people and improved team working. The normalizing of healthy feelings of affection that residential workers have towards children in their care was perhaps the most constructive thing reported. This epitomizes a pedagogy of the heart in which kindness is the primary virtue.

Admittedly, there is still much more fieldwork to be done in social pedagogic projects in the UK before firmer conclusions can be made. It is therefore salutary to heed Kornbeck's (2002, p. 42) sober warning that, 'Social professions in Europe are not purely rational creations which can be remodelled according to a plan based on technicalities'. Social pedagogy always bears the cultural identity of its own history. While this might not pose problems in specific countries, Kornbeck (2002) notes that contextedness may make it difficult to transfer models of social pedagogy from one country to another. Invoking the "chalk and cheese" metaphor, he wonders, and properly so, if the English will be able to adapt to Continental European ways. The "ancestral home" of social pedagogy, Germany, and the aspiring "collector", England, are so unalike in their histories of social professions that a straightforward handover does not seem very realistic.

Yet despite some reservations, Kornbeck (2002) concedes that the English are good at incorporating and modifying "foreign" ideas, such as social pedagogy. In addition, he (2002, p. 46) sensibly concludes that, 'the case of importing SP [Social Pedagogy] to the UK is not one for concern but one for reflection'. It is significant to add that Smith and Whyte (2008) have found traces of social pedagogic practice north of the English border during the Scottish Reformation (c. 1525-1690). This long period of religious reconstruction also ushered in social and economic changes, among them the delegation of responsibility for social welfare to the local parish.

As well as administering poor relief, the Scottish Kirk (Church) became responsible for education. Such melding of care and education is a distinguishing feature of social pedagogic practice. Indeed, Smith & Whyte (2008) go so far as to argue that social pedagogy today reclaims a Scottish tradition. It should also be borne in mind that social pedagogy has been practised in Britain for hundreds of years under whatever title was used to describe charitable kindness to the needy. Notwithstanding, an explicit conception of social pedagogy as a discipline and a field of practice seems only to have appeared in England over the past 30 years or so. But that development is important in itself. It has given social pedagogy a clearer sense of purpose and direction.

There is, of course, a fair bit of catch-up to do because social pedagogic thinking has a longer history in Continental Europe than in the UK. For example, Natorp's (1904) foundational theory has already influenced the development of social pedagogy in Denmark and Sweden. His ideas have also attracted interest in Spain for some time. Furthermore, social pedagogic thinking in Spanish-speaking countries is known to have influenced the development of disciplinary theory in Finland (cf. Hämäläinen, 2003). If the UK politicians do decide to continue the process of importing social pedagogy into care and education policy, care/pedagogic practitioners will need to get used to a new vocabulary. As a consequence, they will have to shed the English habit, already identified by Petrie et al (2006), of conceptualising "pedagogy" in narrowly defined areas, notably, schooling.

Indeed, even the English language itself can create cultural barriers:

> 'Because we rely to such a large extent on translation and interpretation, it is difficult, for English people to recognise ways of thinking which are not possible and ideas that are not thinkable in English but may be important in other traditions' (Petrie & Cameron, 2009, p. 148).

I understand this rejoinder. On my journey of discovery into Continental European social pedagogy, it has not always been easy to find English equivalents for social pedagogic concepts in German and Norwegian texts. The problem has been compounded when trying to make "English sense" of 19th century German, the language in which much of the foundational work in social pedagogy was written. However, because I am fluent in Norwegian, things are easier for me when consulting social pedagogic texts in that language. Even so, Norwegian usage is not always clear-cut. For example, many social pedagogues in Norway are known as "barnevernspedagoger". A very literal English translation of this term is, "child protection pedagogues". However, the use of the word "protection" might convey to English ears a policing or controlling meaning. For this reason, whenever I translate "barnevernspedagoger" into English, I use "child welfare pedagogues". That term expresses, I believe, the more authentic and gentler Nordic rendition.

Linguistic challenges aside, Petrie and Cameron (2009) are surely right to argue that the struggle to understand other ways of looking at the world, as expressed in different languages, is a rewarding exercise. It makes the project of importing social pedagogy worthwhile because English eyes are then opened to different and perhaps better models of care.

On balance then?

So far, but only based on a paucity of research, the picture concerning the exportability of social pedagogy to the UK is equivocal but optimistic. I find that heartening. The national and county projects in England (Cameron et al, 2011; Berridge et al, 2011; Boyce, 2010) might be harbingers of further evaluative research. True, hiccups, setbacks and expressions of concern were reported in the two projects. But such is to be expected in preliminary trials of a discipline largely unheard of in England. For all that, the initial signs are up-beat: social pedagogy has arrived and has been found to offer helpful ideas. If and when the nation incorporates and evaluates more Continental European practice, it will be interesting to see what model or models show promise (or otherwise). Regardless, the hunt for a standard benchmark of best social pedagogic practice, though it may be alluring, could be ill-advised.

Even a cursory look at different European welfare systems – which, if it exists, is where social pedagogy is nested – shows considerable diversity (cf. Esping-Andersen, 2004). This is why it is arguably smart to pore over promising social pedagogic practice in countries that share certain key features with the learner nation, in this case, the UK. For this reason, I think Norway warrants more attention. Like Britons, Norwegians believe that healthcare should be based on clinical need, not ability to pay. Unlike in the UK, though, social pedagogy has a longer and surer footing in Norway, not least in the childcare sector. Yet, on balance, both nations are, as I have pointed out, kindred spirits insofar as universal healthcare is concerned. So there could be good prospects for lesson-drawing from Nordic social pedagogic practice, which, like the health service, is also comprehensive.

Nevertheless, the context specificity "versus" universal application debate must not be over-stated in discussions of lesson-drawing. Social pedagogic practice, wherever it is found, will always contain a mixture of similarities and differences. For example, Norwegian social pedagogy in schools has helped to sustain an informal milieu involving staff and students. In a country like England, where teacher-student relationships are more formalised, particularly in high schools, the Nordic model might be out of place; unless, of course, English educationists wish to adopt a more easy-going approach! But this does not prevent lesson-drawing in other areas, such as, for example, in work with disabled people.

If careful inspection of an overseas intervention bodes well, it would not be unreasonable to apply some lessons in the home setting. At this juncture, however, there looms a balancing act. Uncritical copying is always unwise because it fails to take sufficient account of, at least, some cultural and political differences between countries. On the other hand, a patchy transfer of selected elements is a risky venture too because positive factors in the original intervention can easily be overlooked.

Finding the right weighting is thus a demanding but still a necessary task. Rose (2001) thinks that the best strategy is to concentrate on the general principles rather than on fine grain details. Not to do so, is to risk abstracting a model that is inherently over-deterministic and thereby likely to fail. If, however, the generic principles of an overseas programme are properly mapped and intelligently imported, then the old adage about having to re-invent the (whole) wheel can be avoided. Rose (2001, p. 5) puts his finger on another important matter when he proposes that sensible lesson-drawing across nations is contingent upon finding out to what extent and under what circumstances, 'a programme that works there [will] also work here'.

Pilot work of the kind conducted by Cameron et al (2011) and evaluated by Berridge et al (2011) (see above) on the introduction of social pedagogic practice in English children's homes is prudent. It tests the water before taking the plunge. Such explorative research makes it possible to tap into an invaluable source of practical and useful ideas. Added momentum is gathered when nations adopt similar models and measurements in evidence-based studies. Proximity of this kind increases the chance of arriving at plausible conclusions irrespective of national context. It is therefore reassuring that a raft of recent research has addressed the issue of potential policy transfer in the field of social pedagogy between Continental Europe and England (e.g. Kornbeck, 2006; Petrie & Cameron, 2009; Stephens, 2009).

The conclusions are cautiously buoyant, which is a good sign because it curbs over-enthusiastic but short-sighted mimicking. If the UK is to learn and apply social pedagogic practice of Continental European vintage, then it must do so circumspectly. It is also salutary to recognise that cross-national attraction is a point of departure that does not necessarily predict closing stages (cf. Phillips & Ochs, 2004). Actually, the proof of the pudding is found in a series of stages, the last being pivotal:

1. Identify a problem in the home country

2. Find a similar problem and a successful solution in another country

3. Import the successful policy

4. Adapt and apply it to home circumstances

5. Evaluate the outcome

KEY QUESTION

Evaluating the outcomes of imported ideas is crucial in cross-national lesson-drawing. But how is it possible to evaluate the effectiveness of an imported social programme?

If these steps are followed, it is then possible to see if a borrowed policy works or not (cf. Winther-Jensen, 2011). With regard to evaluation, quantitative and qualitative measurements are both important. That way, number and text are taken into consideration. If, however, as in some studies, statistical analysis is the chosen method, it is helpful to use comparable measurement scales. I can illustrate this point by referring to a quantitative study that is being undertaken by one of my master students in Norway. Let me call him Mark.

This student is conducting research into the relationship between traditional masculine role perceptions and attitudes towards the use of anabolic androgenic steroids. The sample (based on convenience and hence not representative) consists of 28 males aged between 14 and 18 in a Norwegian County. All these adolescents lived in children's homes at the time of the field research, which was carried out in 2011. By way of summary, Mark has found a strong statistical correlation between adolescent male role attitude and attitude towards use of anabolic androgenic steroids. Specifically, the more "macho" the preferred male attitude, the more likely the respondent was found to be liberal towards steroid use. The findings are suggestive rather than comprehensive, but there are paths that can be pursued further. Based on results to date, I have suggested to Mark that he should construct a social pedagogic intervention.

What I have in mind, is a programme that might help these and/or other adolescents to "unlearn" the notion that being macho implies taking steroids at the gym. Sure, they want to increase their muscle mass. But that can be done more safely and, critical this, in an authentic masculine manner by pumping iron. Based on that suggestion, Mark has chosen an appropriate title for his master dissertation: *Real men pump iron*. The objective is not to socialize people into becoming less macho, but rather to be macho, if that is what they want, more safely. This research is in the early stages, and Mark and I do not know where it will finally lead. But if a re-learning programme is produced and tested in one Norwegian county, there is nothing to stop it from being replicated in other counties or even abroad. The important thing is to compare like with like, insofar as this is possible, by using the same research instruments.

My impression is that not enough (if any) of the comparative work on the exportability of social pedagogy from Continental Europe to England has yet used equivalent measurement instruments. To be sure, this is harder to achieve (and not necessarily appropriate) in qualitative studies, but is relatively easy to accomplish in statistical research. So I propose that many systematic replication studies should be carried out in comparative social pedagogy. Once it has been decided to "borrow" a social pedagogic intervention from abroad – for example, the relaxed but purposeful Nordic culture of staff-child relations in children's' homes – it is essential to sift in and sift out promising and unworkable elements. Part of this process might be started prior to programme implementation, but much can also be done along the way on a trial and error basis.

Concluding remarks

I think by now, the reader will have discerned that I am a slightly incredulous but nevertheless hopeful advocate of cross-national lesson-drawing. But I cannot wish into existence what I would like to see! To do so would be fanciful, not scientific. Therefore I place my confidence in recasting successful social projects from abroad into a social pedagogy that the British can learn to live with and, indeed, benefit from. In essence, this implies importing a model that stays within the general parameters of Continental European ways, without being impossible to tell apart.

Finally, I am deeply impressed with the stirring dedication in Rose's (2005) landmark book, *Learning from Comparative Public Policy: A Guide to Analysis*. He dedicates the work to, 'All those who have the imagination and the mettle to search afar for knowledge'.

Chapter 7
Conclusion

Background

In this final chapter, I reflect briefly on the main points in the previous chapters. I have investigated the nature of social pedagogy as a discipline and as a practice, and have commented on its recent and continuing introduction into the UK. In particular, I have emphasised how important it is not to be hasty with practicalities without first exploring social pedagogic theory in more depth. Insofar as social pedagogic practice is concerned, I have argued that the aim is individual and collective change agency in pursuit of self-improvement and social solidarity.

The main vehicles for this objective are social learning of the kind that nurtures the value of social justice and the internalisation of its close cousin, compassion. Along the way, dialogic communication invites us to a field where we can meet as equal discussants. Finally, I have turned my attention to the challenges and opportunities facing policymakers who seek to apply auspicious aspects of best social pedagogic practice abroad in order to improve things in the UK. The introduction of social pedagogy from Continental Europe into a UK setting is proceeding at a fairly rapid pace. Nevertheless, there is still an inadequate understanding of social pedagogic theory in the home nation, which makes it difficult to contemplate meaningful practice. Unless the problem is resolved, social pedagogy will remain tenuously founded on nebulous conjecture and unreflective practice.

Understanding social pedagogy

The recognition that social pedagogy is under-theorised in the UK (Petrie, & Cameron, 2009), lays down a challenge: to scrutinise existing theory and to construct new theory. The two endeavours are not necessarily contrary. For example, a contemporary theory might incorporate classic ideas, while at the same time making refinements based on current thinking and new evidence. By the same token, there will be occasions when foundational and late-modern theories of social pedagogy are perceived as incompatible in some areas. But when all is said and done, the most important criterion of a good theory is that foremost experts in the field assent to its veracity. A helpful starting point is to document and critique social pedagogy's origins. As already made clear, the discipline has a strong German lineage and, in particular, from the mid-19th to the early 20th century. Natorp (1904) looms large here. His conceptualisation of social pedagogy as a discipline that interrogates each of its constituent parts (the social and the pedagogic) is as valid today as it ever was. In fact, that epic formulation has helped me to understand social pedagogy more than anything else.

Like all theories, social pedagogy has its so-called haecceity, its "thisness", or signature, if you will. Sometimes a subject's signature defines a dense, relatively bounded subject area, such as is found in mathematics. Other disciplines, including social pedagogy, have a roomier subject profile. To make this difference clearer, I have constructed two simple tables below. Each table is preceded by a question. The answers **(in bold text)** represent my opinion.

Mathematics has a distinct subject profile

Strongly Agree Agree   Sometimes   Disagree   Strongly Disagree

Social pedagogy has a distinct subject profile

Strongly Agree   Agree   **Sometimes**   Disagree   Strongly Disagree

I chose **Sometimes** for social pedagogy because I have found that its ostensible subject matter attracts quite a lot of different views. It is wise here to note that social pedagogy, like other social sciences, comes in different "shapes and sizes", or at least to an extent (Petrie & Cameron, 2009). Furthermore, social pedagogy, considerably more so than mathematics, is openly multi-disciplinary, which means that it integrates other subjects (e.g. pedagogy, philosophy, psychology and sociology) into its disciplinary space. At the same time, social pedagogy maintains a sort of uniqueness because it is always concerned with the interplay between the social and the educational aspects of life, both defined widely.

At present, social pedagogy is making a partial and a fragmented entry onto British shores. I think that the main culprit behind this piecemeal affair is the lack of attention to social pedagogic theory. One solution lays in good English translations of foundational social pedagogy texts, particularly from Germany, which is where the discipline started in the mid-19th century. That would deepen our understanding of the classic social pedagogic mind-set. The history of social pedagogy from the early

20th century onwards, much of it still German but nevertheless influenced by ideas and practices in other countries, also needs closer scrutiny. New theory building is crucial too.

To undervalue the importance of social pedagogic theory, is to fly by the seat of our pants, which is not an option. More (much more!) systematic theory is the only choice if social pedagogy is to make itself better known in the home nation. Consider, for example, the status of clinical psychology in the UK. The sheer number of psychologists has grown and the discipline has a strong theory-practice anchorage in texts going back to Sigmund Freud (the founder of psychoanalysis) through B. F. Skinner (a founder of behaviourist therapy) and Albert Ellis (the founder of modern behavioural cognitive theory). There are, of course many other eminent clinical psychologists who could be added to this short roll of fame.

Social pedagogy should, I believe, follow a similar path. If it does, the discipline will relinquish its fuzzy identity and present its secrets openly. In the UK, there is every opportunity for social pedagogy to take that road. Indeed, the fact that British social pedagogy is, so to speak, a protégé discipline, bodes well. This allows the project to start from scratch by systematically exploring foundational theory and the later progress of social pedagogic thinking. Although I have emphasised that the main origins of theory are found in 19th century Germany, it is relevant to note that some authors (e.g. Petrie & Cameron, 2009; Smith & Whyte, 2008) have reclaimed an English and a Scottish heritage in social and educational care. Furthermore, they have put a name to it: "social pedagogy". The more this term becomes a part of the English vernacular, the more likely it is for students, practitioners, academics and policymakers to reach a common understanding of the discipline rather than talking past each other.

Such a development would represent **a much-needed corrective** to the current disarray in social pedagogic knowledge, bringing a measure of conceptual unity to theory and practice. Of course, there will be debate, which is good. That stimulates critique and rigour. My point is that there needs to be a working level of common agreement on the basics. If not, there is the risk that (too much) schismatic thinking will compromise the search for unifying concepts. In this pursuit, the development of a provisional definition of social pedagogy is imperative.

Defining social pedagogy: Again?

In his brilliant study of *The Roots of Romanticism* (2000, p. 1), the philosopher, Isaiah Berlin (1909-1997), who was born in Latvia but came to England in 1921, issues a stern warning:

'I might be expected to begin, or to attempt to begin, with some kind of definition of romanticism, or at least some generalisation, in order to make clear what it is that I mean by it. I do not propose to walk into that particular trap.'

Berlin (2000) then proceeds to explain his caginess regarding definitions. In essence, his argument is that there are too many countervailing strands in romantic thought, which makes it impossible to discern what romanticism has in common. Point taken! Notwithstanding, I find some solace in Kornbeck's view (2009, p. 211) – and now I am referring to social pedagogy, not romanticism – that:

'social pedagogy is so much a concept in its own right that it deserves having its own discourse at European level, rather than being occasionally mentioned whenever unspecified 'social work' is compared.'

Precisely, Jacob Kornbeck! To reiterate, leaving social pedagogy undefined, is to remain in Weber's (1949, p. 94) exasperating 'realm of the vaguely "felt"; and I do not wish to leave you there, dear reader, certainly not in a textbook of social pedagogy. So with no disrespect to Professor Berlin, a man of towering intellect, I do choose to define my discipline because social pedagogy does have its own frame of reference. It is important to add that, unlike romanticism, which represents, in various forms, a revolution of huge proportions, social pedagogy confines itself to a more specific problem, namely, the interplay between the social and the pedagogic in society.

As a professor of social pedagogy, I often have to explain what it is that I study. I still find this daunting. But, having raised a thorny issue, it is incumbent on me to offer clarification. In Chapter 1, I offered Hämäläinen's (2003, p. 71) definition of social pedagogy as a helpful starting point. In order to jog the memory, here it is again:

'Historically, social pedagogy is based on the belief that you can decisively influence social circumstances through education'.

In chapter 2, I presented Natorp's (1904, p. 94) classic definition of social pedagogy:

I still think Natorp's (1904) definition is as good as it gets. Notwithstanding, in the same chapter, I proposed my own definition of social pedagogy, and here it is, just to remind you:

Social pedagogy is the social scientific study of planned and impromptu socialisation via the social learning and the emotional internalisation of values and norms.

Typically, in planned socialisation, social pedagogues seek to enable perceived self- and group efficacy so that people can change their lives and society for the better. In most cases, planning and execution are decided through respectful dialogue involving the social pedagogue and the individual or the group. The aim is to reach agreement on a workable course of action.

There is a crucial rejoinder. Individuals and groups are at liberty to plan their own socialisation to varying degrees by choosing how to live their own lives. At that juncture, the social pedagogue's role is to step back.

For now, I am content (not quite the right word, but please indulge me!) to let my definition stand on a provisional basis. I sincerely invite you, the reader, to critique and discuss it; and I have no doubt that, at some point, I will have to make changes, perhaps based on your suggestions.

From theory to practice

From sound theory, flows informed action. Too often, I have found that social pedagogy is presented as an almost theory-free practice. This is worrying but telling. The guiding idea behind social pedagogic practice therefore needs to be stated. It is this: human beings can be educated to have a hand in shaping the social environment in which they live, provided they believe they can do so. Once this self- and collective efficacy is admitted, people can prevent social problems from arising, as well as solving the social problems they face. That capacity gains added impetus when people choose to improve their lives through united effort. The valued life path in Continental European social pedagogic practice is the path that commits to social justice for all.

This is the theoretical (and ethical) reference point of the social pedagogic project in late-modern society. Its realisation is contingent upon an education into social life, as well as the internalisation of co-operative dispositions. In addition, there is the need for an assured sense of own and other's capacity and worth, which is then acted on. The job of the social pedagogue is that of educational enabler, whether this involves nurturing personal and collective capacities and/or, as appropriate, by providing by-proxy support. Those functions constitute the crux of social pedagogic practice.

Even though it might be argued that by-proxy support undermines the rallying of efficacy beliefs, I disagree. Sure, from a purely pedagogic standpoint, by-proxy support is more of a functional manoeuvre than an educational intervention. However, because, as I have consistently argued, private troubles are connected to public issues (Mills, 2000), social pedagogues must advocate on behalf of the poor. How else can socially disadvantaged people be expected to mobilise their own efficacy when insuperable structural obstacles get in the way? Once the empirical link between personal biography and social structure is unveiled, social pedagogic practice can place itself in the service of social justice. Note the unity of empirical and normative motivation here, a condition beautifully captured in Martin Luther Kings's (1964; no pagination) turn of phrase, 'bright-eyed wisdom'.

In practical terms, social pedagogic solutions are found in the re-learning of values and norms, the aim being to develop a more critical social literacy. This pedagogy of the oppressed (cf. Freire, 1996a), when understood and felt, is a powerful mover of change. It encourages people to shift their outlook so that they can understand their predicament and take positive steps to change it. In addition, the conversion of efficacious belief into collective purpose helps tilt the balance of power in society more in favour of these who have least.

Among the most important social pedagogic tools to get the job done, are "mastery learning" and "scaffolding": the first being the assignment of paced learning tasks, the second (and related instrument) the providing of support to novice learners so as to enhance mastery. Additionally, social pedagogues must enlist in dogged advocacy in the cause of social justice. Yes, this will, at times, entail coping with exasperation, mainly with bureaucratic elites, but sometimes with service users too. More importantly, however, social pedagogic practice calls upon excellent lobbying skills and an impeccable knowledge of service user rights. But fighting for social justice with and on behalf of the socially disadvantaged brings rewards. Each little victory carries vicarious joy to the social pedagogue, which is its own prize.

Afterthought

In this book, I have laid bare the bold outlines of social pedagogy. My aim has been to show how the study of socialisation for social justice can be applied in the real world. In concrete terms, this necessitates the building of a kinder and a gentler society for people to live and interact in.

It is up to the transfer agents of cross-national lesson-drawing in the UK to decide, in conjunction with policymakers, the lessons they want to draw from social pedagogy in Continental Europe. The process has already begun and is starting to show some beneficial effects. However, things are still too localised and fragmented at present. So there remains a challenge. Stated directly, it is this: to find and implement social pedagogic thinking and practice that is ambitious for the well-being of every child and adult in society.

Some of you will be doing social pedagogic work already, but perhaps you have not yet put a name to what you do. If what you practise feels like social pedagogy, then it might be; but, then again, it might not be. Now that you have read this book, it is time to take stock. That will give you a surer footing in social pedagogy regardless of your background.

References

Abbott, G. (1917). *The Immigrant And The Community*. New York: The Century Co.

Adler, M. J. (1941). Are There Absolute and Universal Principles on Which Education Should be Founded? In M. J. Adler. (1990). *Reforming Education*. (pp. 53-65). New York: Collier Books.

Adler, M. J. (1987). Teaching, Learning, and Their Counterfeits In M. J. Adler. (1990). *Reforming Education*. (pp. 167-175). New York: Collier Books

Allport, G. W. (1979). *The Nature of Prejudice*. New York: Basic Books.

Andersen, G. E. (2002). Towards the Good Society, Once Again? In G. E. Andersen, D. Gallie, A. Hemerijck & J. Myles (Eds.), *Why We Need a New Welfare State*. (pp. 1-25). Oxford: Oxford University Press.

Aristotle (originally written in 350 B.C.E.), *Nichomachean Ethics*. This translated English version accessed from The Internet Classics Archive on 13 August 2012 at: http://classics.mit.edu/Aristotle/nichomachaen.1.i.html

Arnstein, S. R. (1969). A Ladder of Citizen Participation, *Journal of the American Planning Association*, *35*, 4, 216-224.

Bandura, A. (1982). Self-Efficacy Mechanism in Human Agency, *American Psychologist*, *37*, 2, 122-147.

Bandura, A. (1997). *Self-Efficacy*. New York: W. H. Freeman and Company.

Bartsch, A. (2004). *Emotional communication – a theoretical model*. Paper for the 9th IGEL Conference. Edmonton, Canada, August 3-7, 2004.

Bauman, Z. (2003). *Liquid Love*. Cambridge and Oxford: Polity Press in association with Blackwell Publishing Ltd.

Bauman, Z. (2007). *Work, consumerism and the new poor*. 2nd Edition. Maidenhead: Open University Press.

Bauman, Z. (2009). *Postmodern Ethics*. Malden, MA: Blackwell Publishing.

Bell, B. & Yarborough, E. (2003). Don't Take "No" for an Answer. In A. Nash (Ed.), *Civic Participation and Community Action Sourcebook*. (p. 141). Boston, MA: New England Literary Resource Center.

Bensing J. M. & Dronkers J.(1992). Instrumental and affective aspects of physician behaviour, *Medical Care*, *20*, 4, 283-298.

Berlin, I. (2000). *The Roots of Romanticism*. London: Pimlico.

Bernstein, B. (1999). Vertical and Horizontal Discourse: an essay, *British Journal of Sociology of Education*, *20*, 2, 157-173.

Bernstein, B. (2000). *Pedagogy, Symbolic Control and Identity*. Revised Edition. Lanham, Maryland: Rowman & Littlefield Publishers, Inc.

Berridge, D., Biehal, N., Lutman, E. & Palomares, L. H. M. (2011). *Raising the bar? Evaluation of the Social Pedagogy Pilot Programme in residential children's homes.* Research Report DFE-RR148. London: Department for Education.

Beugre, C. (2010). Resistance to Socialization into Organizational Corruption: A Model of Deontic Justice, *Journal of Business Psychology, 25*, 533-541.

Beveridge, Sir William. (1942). *Social Insurance And Allied Services.* London: His Majesty's Stationary Office.

Bourdieu, P. (1999). *The Weight of the World.* Cambridge & Oxford: Polity Press in association with Blackwell Publishers Ltd.

Bourdieu, P. (2004). *Acts of Resistance.* Cambridge: Polity Press.

Bowlby, J. (2005). *A Secure Base.* Routledge: NewYork.

Boyce, N. (2010). Social Pedagogy in Essex. *Children Webmag.* Accessed 9 April 2012 at: http://www.childrenwebmag.com/articles/social-pedagogy/social-pedagogy-in-essex

Bringuier, J.-C. (1990). *Conversations with Jean* Piaget. Chicago: The University of Chicago Press.

Bru, E., Stephens P. & Torsheim, T. (2002). Students' Perceptions of Class Management and Reports of Their Own Misbehavior, *Journal of School Psychology, 40*, 4, 287-307.

Bruner, J. (1996). *The Culture of Education.* Cambridge, Massachusetts: Harvard University Press.

Bruner, J. (1977). *The Process of Education.* Cambridge, Massachusetts: Harvard University Press.

Buber, M. (1997). Martin Buber. In C. Rogers (1997). *Carl Rogers: Dialogues.* (pp. 41-63). Edited by H. Kirschenbaum & V. L. Henderson. London: Constable and Company Ltd.

Buber, M. (2004). *I and Thou.* London: Continuum.

Burke, E. (1770). *Thoughts on the cause of the present discontents.* 3rd Edition. London: J. Dodsley.

Böhnisch, L. & Schröer, W. (2011). Social Pedagogy of the Life Stages. In J. Kornbeck & N. Rosendal Jensen (Eds.), *Social Pedagogy for the Entire Lifespan.* Volume XV. (pp. 16-28). Bremen: Europäischer Hochschulverlag GmbH & Co. KG.

Cameron, C. (2004). Social Pedagogy and Care: Danish and German Practice in Young People's Residential Care, *Journal of Social Work, 4*, 2, 133-151.

Cameron, C., Jasper, A., Kleipoedszus, S., Petrie, P. & Wigfall, V. (2010). *Implementing the DCSF Pilot Programme: The work of the first year Social Pedagogy Briefing Paper II.* London: Thomas Coram Research Unit, Institute of Education, University of London.

Cameron, C., Petrie, P., Wigfall, V., Kleipoedszus, S., Jasper, A. (2011). *Final report of the social pedagogy pilot programme: development and implementation.* London: Thomas Coram Research Unit, Institute of Education, University of London.

Center for the Study and Prevention of Violence (CSPV). (2007). *Blueprints for Violence Prevention Overview.* University of Colorado at Boulder. Accessed 17 June 2007 at: http://www.colorado.edu/cspv/blueprints/index.html

Chapman, L. & West-Burnham, J. (2010). *Education for Social Justice.* London: Continuum International Publishing Group.

Coussée, F., Bradt, L., Roose, R. & Bouverne-De Bie, M. (2010). The Emerging Social Pedagogical Paradigm in UK Child and Youth Care: Deus Ex Machina or Walking the Beaten Path?, *British Journal of Social Work, 40*, 789-805.

Curry, P., De Amicis, L. & Gilligan, R. (2010). *Protocol: Effects of Cooperative Learning on Inter Ethnic Relations in School Settings.* The Campbell Collaboration.

Darwin, C. (1874; republished 2007). *The Descent of Man.* Forgotten Books: *www.forgottenbooks.org*

DCSF [Department for Children, Schools & Families]. (2007). *The Children's Plan.* London: DCSF.

DCSF [Department for Children, Schools & Families]. (2008). *2020 Children and Young People's Workforce Strategy.* London: DCSF.

DfES [Department for Education & Skills]. (2003). *Every Child Matters.* London: DfES.

Durkheim, E. (1980). Pedagogy and sociology. In B. R. Cosin, I. R. Dale, G. M. Esland, D. Mackinnon & D. F. Swift (Eds.), *School and Society: A Sociological Reader*, 2nd Edition. (pp. 79–83). London: Routledge & Kegan Paul. London.

Durkheim, E. (1994). *On Institutional Analysis* (edited, translated and with an introduction by M. Traugott). Chicago: The University of Chicago Press.

Dworkin, P. H. (2003). Preventive Health Care and Anticipatory Guidance. In J. P. Shonkoff & S. J. Meisels (Eds.), *Handbook of Early Childhood Intervention.* 2nd Edition. (pp. 327-338). Cambridge: Cambridge University Press.

Dworkin, R. (2011). *Justice for Hedgehogs.* Cambridge, Massachusetts: Belknap Press of Harvard University Press.

Esping-Andersen, G. (2004). *The Three Worlds of Welfare Capitalism.* Cambridge and Oxford : Polity Press in association with Blackwell Publishing Ltd.

Esping-Andersen, G. & Myles, J. (no date). *The Welfare State and Redistribution*, no pagination. Accessed 19 January 2012 at: http://dcpis.upf.edu/~gosta-esping-andersen/materials/welfare_state.pdf

Etzioni, A. (2002). Foreword. In N. Gilbert. *Transformation of the Welfare State: The Silent Surrender of Public Responsibility*. Oxford: Oxford University Press.

Foucault, M. (1972). *The Archaeology of Knowledge & The Discourse on Language*. New York: Pantheon Books.

Foucault, M. (1990). *The Use of Pleasure*. New York: Vintage Books.

Foucault, M. (1994). *Ethics: Subjectivity and Truth*. Volume 1. London: Penguin Books Ltd.

Foucault, M. (2008). *The Archaeology of Knowledge*. London: Routledge.

Freire, P. (1996a). *Pedagogy of the Oppressed*. London: Penguin Books Ltd.

Freire, P. (1996b). *Letters to Cristina*. New York: Routledge.

Freire, P. (2006). *Pedagogy of Hope*. London: Continuum.

Freire, P. (2007). *Education for Critical Consciousness*. London: Continuum.

Friesen, N. & Sævi, T. (2010). Reviving forgotten connections in North American teacher education: Klaus Mollenhauer and the pedagogical relation, *Journal of Curriculum Studies*, 1-25. ISSN 0022–0272 print/ISSN 1366–5839 online ©2010 Taylor & Francis, http://www.informaworld.com, DOI: 10.1080/00220270903494279

Fugelli, P. (6 June, 2011). Rød, grøn eller blå resept? (Red, green or blue prescription?; in Norwegian), *Stavanger Aftenblad* [a Norwegian newspaper], p. 3.

Grunwald, K. & Thiersch, H. (2009). The concept of the 'lifeworld orientation' for social work and social care, *Journal of Social Work Practice*, *23*, 2, 131-146.

Günther, K-H. (1993). Friedrich Adolph Wilhem Diesterweg (1790-1866), *PROSPECTS: the quarterly review of comparative education*, *23*, 1/2, 293-302. Paris, UNESCO: International Bureau of Education.

Habermas, J. (1979). *Communication and the Evolution of Society*. Boston: Beacon Press.

Habermas, J. (1984). *The Theory of Communicative Action*. Volume 1. Boston, Massachusetts: Beacon Press

Habermas, J. (1999). *Between Facts and Norms*. Cambridge, Massachusetts: The MIT Press.

Habermas, J. (2005). *The Future of Human Nature*. Cambridge: Polity Press.

Hajek, P., Stead, L. F., West, R., Jarvis, M. & Lancaster, T. (2009). *Relapse prevention interventions for smoking cessation*. Issue 1, Art. No.: CD003999. Cochrane Database of Systematic Reviews.

Halpern, R. (2003). Early Childhood Intervention for Low-Income Children and Families. In J. P. Shonkoff & S. J. Meisels (Eds.), *Handbook of Early Childhood Intervention*. 2nd Edition. (pp. 361-386). Cambridge: Cambridge University Press.

Hannon, C., Wood, C. & Bazalgette, L. (2010). *In Loco Parentis*. London: Demos.

Herrmann, P. (2005). Empowerment: The Core of Social Quality, *European Journal of Social Quality*, 5, 1/2, 289-299.

Herrmann, P. & van der Maesen, L. J. G. (2008). *Social Quality and Precarity: Approaching New Patterns of Societal (Dis-) Integration*. Working Paper nr. 1. The Hague: European Foundation on Social Quality.

Herrmann, P. (2011). The Lifespan Perspective in Comparative Social Policy Research: a Critique of Gøsta Esping-Andersen's Model of Three Welfare States and its Implications for European Comparisons in Social Pedagogy. In J. Kornbeck and N. Rosendal Jensen (Eds.). *Social Pedagogy for the Entire Lifespan*, Volume XV. (pp. 29-49). Bremen: Europäischer Hochschulverlag.

Hämäläinen, J. (1989). Social Pedagogy as a Meta-Theory of Social Work Education, *International Journal of Social Work*, 32, 2, 117-128.

Hämäläinen, J. (2003). The Concept of Social Pedagogy in the Field of Social Work, *Journal of Social Work*, 3, 1, 69-80.

Hämäläinen, J. (2005). Developing social pedagogy as an academic discipline. In H-U Otto & H. Thiersch (Eds.). *Handbuch Sozialarbeit/Sozialpädagogik*. [*Handbook of Social Work/Social Pedagogy*; in German] 3. Auflage. (pp. 133-153). München: Reinhardt EV.

International Commission for the Study of Communication Problems. (1978). *Interim Report on Communication Problems in Modern Society*. Paris.

Jackson, R. (2006). The role of social pedagogy in the training of residential child care workers, *Journal of Intellectual Disabilities*, DOI: 10. 1177/1744629506062275, pp. 61-73.

Jalaludin R. Cited by M. Collopy. (2000, p. 109). *Architects of Peace*. Novato, California: New World Library.

Jones, F. (2006). Strategies to enhance chronic disease self-management: How can we apply this to stroke? *Disability and Rehabilitation*, 28 (13-14), 841 – 847.

Kant, Immanuel (1st published 1785, 1993). *Grounding for the Metaphysics of Morals*. 3rd Edition. Indianapolis: Hackett Publishing Company, Inc.

King, M. L. (1964). *Nobel Lecture: The Quest for Peace and Justice*. Downloaded 29 April 2012 at:
http://www.nobelprize.org/nobel_prizes/peace/laureates/1964/king-lecture.html

King, M. L. (1969). *Chaos or Community?* Harmondsworth: Penguin Books Ltd.

King, M. L. (2007). *The Words and Inspiration of Martin Luther King, JR*. Auckland, New Zealand: PQ Blackwell Limited.

Kloppenburg, R. & Hendriks, P. (Eds.) (2010). *Outreach Approaches in an International Perspective: Social Work*. Utrecht: Hogeschool Utrecht, Centre of Social Innovation.

Knapp, M., McDaid, D. & Parsonage, M. (2011). *Mental health promotion and prevention: The economic case*. London: Department of Health.

Kornbeck, J. (2006). Reflections on the Exportability of Social Pedagogy and its Possible Limits, *Social Work in Europe*, 9, 2, 37–49.

Kornbeck, J. (2009). 'Important but Widely Misunderstood': the problem of defining social pedagogy in Europe. In J. Kornbeck & N. Rosendal Jensen (Eds.), *The Diversity of Social Pedagogy in Europe*. Volume VII. (pp. 211-235). Bremen: Europäischer Hochschulverlag GmbH & Co. KG.

Kornbeck, J. & Rosendal Jensen, N. (2011). Social Pedagogy – Not only for Infants, Orphans and Young People. In J. Kornbeck & N. Rosendal Jensen (Eds.), *Social Pedagogy for the Entire Lifespan*. Volume XV. (pp. 1-14). Bremen: Europäischer Hochschulverlag GmbH & Co. KG.

Kornbeck, J. (2012). *Transatlanticism Reloaded*. William Thompson Working Papers, 23. University of Cork. NB. The William-Thompson-Working-Paper-Series is edited by the European Social Organisational and Science Consultancy for the University of Cork, Department of Applied Social Studies. The work is edited and supervised for publication by Professor Peter Herrmann, ESOSC.

Kozol, J. (1986). *Illiterate America*. New York: Penguin Books USA Inc.

Kozol, J. (1993). *On Being a Teacher*. Oxford: Oneworld Publications Ltd.

Kroll, J. & Bachrach, B. (1986). Child Care and Child Abuse in Early Medieval Europe, *Journal of the American Academy of Child Psychiatry*, 25, 4, 562-568.

Lakoff, G. (2002). *Moral Politics*. Chicago: The University of Chicago Press.

Lave, J. & Wenger, E. (2003). *Situated Learning: Legitimate peripheral participation*. Cambridge: Cambridge University Press.

Lazarus, R. S. & Folkman, S. (1984). *Stress, Appraisal, and Coping*. New York: Springer Publishing Company.

Lazarus, R. S. (1993). Coping Theory and Research: Past, Present, and Future. *Psychosomatic Medicine, 55*, 234-247.

Levinas, E. (1991). *Totality and Infinity*. Dordrecht, The Netherlands: Kluwer Academic Publishers.

Levinas, E., Bradley Smith, M. & Harshav, B. (2006). *Entre Nous*. London: Continuum.

Lewin, K. (1951). *Field theory in social science; selected theoretical papers*. New York: Harper & Row.

Lewin, K. (2000). *Resolving Social Conflicts & Field Theory in Social Science*. Washington DC: American Psychological Association.

Lewis, H. (2003). *For the Common Good*. Edited by M. Reisch. New York: Brunner-Routledge.

Limber, S. P., Nation, M., Tracy, A. J., Melton, G. B. & Flerx, V. (2004). Implementation of the Olweus Bullying Prevention program in the Southeastern United States. In P. K. Smith, D. Pepler & K. Rigby (Eds.), *Bullying in Schools: How Successful Can Interventions Be?* (pp. 55-79).

Cambridge: Cambridge University Press.

Lipsky, M. (1980). *Street-Level Bureaucracy.* New York: Russell Sage Foundation.

Lorenz, W. (2004). *Towards a European paradigm of social work – Studies in the history of modes of social work and social policy in Europe.* Doctor of Philosophy Thesis, Technical University of Dresden.

Lorenz, W. (2008). Paradigms and Politics: Understanding Methods Paradigms in an Historical Context: The Case of Social Pedagogy, *British Journal of Social Work,* 38, 4, 625-644.

Marmot, M. (2006). Introduction. In M. Marmot & R. Wilkinson (Eds.). *Social Determinants of Health.* 2nd Edition. (pp. 1-5). Oxford: Oxford University Press.

Masten, A. S. (2001). Ordinary Magic: Resilience Processes in Development, *American Psychologist,* 56, 3, 227-238.

Mathiesen, R. (1999). An examination of the theoretical foundation of social pedagogy, *The Journal of the European Association of Training Centres for Socio-Educational Casework,* 3, 3–27.

Mathiesen, R. (2008). *Sosialpedagogisk Perspektiv på Individ og Fellesskap* (*The Social Pedagogic View of Individual and Cooperative Spirit*; in Norwegian). Oslo: Universitetsforlaget.

Meisels, S. J. & Shonkoff, J. P. (2003). Early Childhood Intervention: A Continuing Evolution. In J. P. Shonkoff & S. J. Meisels (Eds.), *Handbook of Early Childhood Intervention.* 2nd Edition. (pp. 3-31). Cambridge: Cambridge University Press.

Miller, D. (1999). *Principles of Social Justice.* Cambridge, Massachusetts: Harvard University Press.

Mills, C. Wright. (1973). *The Power Elite.* London: Oxford University Press.

Mills, C. Wright. (2000). *The Sociological Imagination.* Fortieth Anniversary Edition. Oxford: Oxford University Press.

Mollenhauer, K. (1983). *Vergessene Zusammenhänge: über Kultur und Erziehung* [*Forgotten Connections: On Culture and Upbringing*; in German] Munich: Juventa.

Moss, P. & Petrie P. (2002). *From Children's Services to Children's Spaces.* London. Routledge-Falmer.

Moss, P. (3 February, 2010). Analysis: Five steps to better provision, *Nursery World.* No pagination.

Natorp, P. (1904). *Sozialpädagogik. Theorie der Willenserziehung auf der Grundlage der Gemeinschaft* [*Social Pedagogy: the Theory of Community Will*; in German]. Stuttgart: Fr. Frommann Verlag (E. Hauff).

Nordic Campbell Centre (2008). Personal assistance offers people with impairments choice of service and greater quality of life. Accessed on 4 June 2011 at: *www.campbellcollaboration.org/lib/download/174/*

Normann, T. M. (2011). *Materielle og sosiale mangler: Utslag av fattigdom* (*Material and social deprivations: the impact of poverty*; in Norwegian). Oslo: Statistisk sentralbyrå.

Norwegian Ministry of Education and Norwegian Ministry of Children & Families. (2000). *Vurdering av program og tiltak for å redusere problematferd og utvikle sosial kompetanse* [*Evaluation of programmes and initiatives to reduce problem behaviour and to develop social competence*; in Norwegian]. Oslo.

Norwegian Ministry of Education and Norwegian Ministry of Children & Families. (2005). *Rammeplan og Forskrift for 3-Årig Barnevernspedagogutdanning* [*National Framework and Regulations for the 3-Year Education of Child Welfare Pedagogues*; in Norwegian]. Utdannings- og forskningsdepartem entet, Oslo.

NOU [Official Norwegian Reports]. (2009). *Kompetanseutvikling i barnevernet* [*Competence Development in the Child Welfare Service*; in Norwegian]. Oslo: Akademika AS, Avdeling for offentlige publikasjoner.

Olweus, D. (2001) *Olweus' Kjerneprogram mot Mobbing og Antisosial Atferd: En Lærerveiledning* [Olweus's core programme against bullying and antisocial behaviour: a teacher handbook], Version III (Bergen).

Olweus Gruppen (The Olweus Group). (2004). *The Olweus Bullying Prevention Program.* One of a series of documents provided by Dan Olweus in conjunction with his paper, *Importance of Monitoring and Evaluation in Program Implementation*, International Policy and Research Conference on School Bullying and Violence, Stavanger, Norway, 7 September, 2004.

Parsons, T. (1938). The Role of Theory in Social Research, *American Sociological Review*, *3*, 1, 13-20.

Parsons, T. (1968). The Theory of Action. In T. Parsons, *The Structure of Social Action: A Study in Social Theory With Special Reference to a Group of Recent European Writers*, Volume 1. (pp. 43-86). New York: Free Press.

Petrie, P., Boddy, J., Cameron, C., Wigfall, V. & Simon, A. (2006). *Working with Children in Care.* Maidenhead: Open University Press.

Petrie, P. & Cameron, C. (2009). Importing Social Pedagogy? In J. Kornbeck & N. Rosendal Jensen (Eds.), *The Diversity of Social Pedagogy in Europe.* Volume VII. (pp. 145-168). Bremen: Europäischer Hochschulverlag GmbH & Co. KG.

Phillips, A. & Taylor, B. (2009). *On Kindness.* London: Hamish Hamilton.

Phillips, D. & Ochs, K. (2004). Researching policy borrowing: some methodological challenges in comparative education, *British Educational Research Journal*, *30*, 6, 773-784.

Popkewitz, T. S. (no date) *The Idea of Science as Planning Was Not Planned: A Historical Note about American Pedagogical Sciences as Planning Society and Individuality*, no pagination. The University of Wisconsin-Madison. Accessed 14 July 2008 at: http://www.ped.gu.se/biorn/popkewitz.pdf

Popper, K. (2007). *The Logic of Scientific Discovery.* Abindon, Oxon: Routledge.

Prange, K. (2004) *Bildung*: a paradigm regained? *European Educational Research Journal*, 3, 501–509.

Pugh, R. & Richards, M. (1996). Speaking out: A practical approach to empowerment, *Practice*, 8, 2, 35-44.

Rawls, J. (2003). *A Theory of Justice*. Revised Edition. Cambridge, Massachusetts: The Belknap Press of Harvard University Press.

Reisch, M. & Andrews, J. (2002). *The Road Not Taken*. New York: Brunner-Routledge.

Rigoni, Padre F. M. (2007). Compassion and Solidarity. In S. Dumont and M. St-Onge (Eds.). (pp. 17-27). *Social Work, Health, and International Development*: *Compassion in Social Policy and Practice*: Binghamton, NY: Haworth Press.

Rogers, C. (1958). The Characteristics of a Helping Relationship, *Personnel & Guidance Journal*, 37, 1, 6-16.

Rogers, C. (1967). Chapter Six of *The Therapeutic Relationship With Schizophrenics*, by C. R. Rogers, E. T. Gendlin, D. J. Kiesler & C. B. Truax (Eds.). Madison: University of Wisconsin Press. Downloaded 5 February 2012 at: http://www.centerfortheperson.org/pdf/1967__Therapeutic_Conditions_Antecedent_to_Change.pdf

Rogers, C. (1997). *Carl Rogers: Dialogues*. Edited by H. Kirschenbaum & V. L. Henderson. London: Constable and Company Ltd.

Roland, E. & Sørensen Vaaland, G. (2003). *Zero, SAFs program mot mobbing*: *Lærerveiledning* (*Zero, SAF's anti-bullying programme: a Teacher's Guide*; in Norwegian). 2nd Edition. Stavanger: Centre for Behavioural Research, Stavanger University College.

Roosevelt, F. D. (20 January 1941). Third Inaugural Address. Online by Gerhard Peters and John T. Woolley, *The American Presidency Project*. http://www.presidency.ucsb.edu/ws/?pid=16022. No pagination.

Rose, R. (2001). Ten steps in learning lessons from abroad. *Future Governance Paper 1*. Glasgow: University of Strathclyde.

Rosenberg, M. B. (no date; no pagination). *Compassionate Communication*. Accessed 3 February 2012 at: http://www.listeningway.com/compassion.html

Rosenberg, M. B. (2003). *Non-Violent Communication: A Language for Life*. Encintas, CA: PuddleDancer.

Royal Norwegian Ministry of Labour and Social Inclusion. (2009). *Action Plan against Poverty – Status 2008 and intensified efforts 2009*. Oslo

Salmivalli, C., Kaukiainen, A., Voeten, M. & Sinisammal, M. (2004). Targeting the group as a whole: the Finnish anti-bullying intervention. In P. K. Smith, D. Pepler & K. Rigby (Eds.), *Bullying in Schools: How Successful Can Interventions Be?* (pp. 251-273). Cambridge: Cambridge University Press.

Sandel, M. J. (2010). *Justice*. London: Penguin Books Ltd.

The Scottish Government. (2003). *Life In Low Income Families In Scotland: A Review Of The Literature.* Chapter 3 (no pagination). Edinburgh.

Schram, S. F. (2006). *Welfare Discipline.* Philadelphia PA: Temple University Press.

Shaffer, D. R. (2009). *Social and Personality Development.* 6th Edition. Wadsworth, CA: Cengage Learning.

Shim, S. H. (2008). A philosophical investigation of the role of teachers: A synthesis of Plato, Confucius, Buber, and Freire, *Teaching and Teacher Education, 24,* pp. 515–535.

Slife, B. (2005). Testing the Limits of Henriques' Proposal: Wittgensteinian Lessons and Hermeneutic Dialogue, *Journal of Clinical Psychology, 61,* 1, 107-120.

Smith, M. & Whyte, B. (2008). Social education and social pedagogy: reclaiming a Scottish tradition in social work, *European Journal of Social Work, 11,* 1, 15-28.

Smith, M. K. (2009). Social pedagogy. In *The Encyclopaedia of Informal Education,* no pagination. Accessed 30 September 2010 at: http://www.infed.org/biblio/b-socped.htm

Smith, P. K. & Shu, S. (2000). What Good Schools can do about Bullying: Findings from a survey in English schools after a decade of research and action, *Childhood, 7,* 2, 193-212.

Snyder, C. L. & Shane, J. L. (Eds.). (2002). *Handbook of Positive Psychology.* Oxford: Oxford University Press.

Stead, L. F., Bergson, G. & Lancaster, T. (2008). *Physician advice for smoking cessation.* Issue 2, Art. No.: CD000165. Cochrane Database of Systematic Reviews.

Stephens, P. (2009). The nature of social pedagogy: an excursion into Norwegian territory, *Child & Family Social Work, 14,* 343-351.

Stephens, P. (2011a). Preventing and confronting school bullying: a comparative study of two national programmes in Norway, *British Educational Research Journal, 37,* 3, 381-404.

Stephens, P. (2011b). Social pedagogic values in the education of child welfare pedagogues in Norway. In J. Kornbeck and N. Rosendal Jensen (Eds.). *Social Pedagogy for the Entire Lifespan,* Volume XV. (pp. 177-195). Bremen: Europäischer Hochschulverlag.

Stephens, P. (2012). Social Pedagogic Practice: exploring the core. In J. Kornbeck & N. Rosendal Jensen (Eds.), *Social Pedagogy for the Entire Lifespan.* Volume XVIII. (pp. 201-226). Bremen: Europäischer Hochschulverlag GmbH & Co. KG.

Stoltenberg, J., Flåthen, R., Lundby-Wedin, W. et al. (31 January 2012). Den Nordiske modellen for framtida [The Nordic model for the future; in Norwegian], *Dagbladet* [a Norwegian newspaper], p. 50.

Stone, D. (2000). *Learning Lessons, Policy Transfer and the International Diffusion of Policy Ideas*. Centre for the Study of Globalisation and Regionalisation. Jerusalem: Hebrew University of Jerusalem.

Swartz, R. (2007). Social Work Values in an Age of Complexity, *Journal of Social Work Values and Ethics*, 4, 3, (no pagination).

Sylva, K., Melhuish, E., Sammons, P., Siraj-Blatchford, I. & Taggart, B. (2004). *The Effective Provision of Pre-School Education (EPPI) Project: Findings from pre-school to end of Key Stage 1*. Nottingham: DfES Publications.

Sünker, H. & Otto, H.-U. (1997). Foreword. In H. Sünker & H.-U. Otto (Eds.). (pp. vii-viii). *Education and Fascism: Political Identity and Social Education in Nazi Germany*. London: Falmer Press.

Sünker, H. & Braches-Chyrek, R. (2009). Social Pedagogy in Germany. In J. Kornbeck & N. Rosendal Jensen (Eds.). *The Diversity of Social Pedagogy in Europe*. Volume VII. (pp. 12-33). Bremen: Europäischer Hochschulverlag GmbH & Co. KG.

Thomas, E. M. (2004). *Aggressive Behavior Outcomes for Young Children: Change in Parenting Environment Predicts Change in Behavior*. Ottawa: Statistics Canada.

Thoreau, H. D. (1993). *Civil Disobedience and other Essays*. Mineola, NY: Dover Publications, Inc.

Titmuss, R. (1997). *The Gift Relationship*. New York: The New Press.

Tönnies, F. (2009). *Community and Civil Society*. Cambridge: Cambridge University Press.

Unger, R. B. (1987). *Plasticity into Power*. Cambridge: Cambridge University Press.

Utdannings- og forskningsdepartementet. (2005). *Rammeplan og Forskrift for 3-Årig Barnevernspedagogutdanning* [*National Framework and Regulations for the 3-Year Education of Child Welfare Pedagogues*; in Norwegian]. Oslo: Utdannings- og forskningsdepartementet.

The Veterans Site (2012). Accessed on 6 April 2012 at: http://www.thehungersite.com/clickToGive/home.faces;jsessionid=4499CD212 4AF7DC436FD3D7EEF581F22.ctg-c?siteId=10&link=ctg_vet_home_from_ths_home_sitenav

von Goethe, J. W. (2001). *Wilhelm Meister's Apprenticeship*. New York City: Bartleby. com, Inc.

Vygotsky, L. S. (1978). *Mind in Society*. Cambridge, Massachusetts: Harvard University Press.

Webb, S. A. (2007). The comfort of strangers: social work, modernity and late Victorian England – Part II, *European Journal of Social Work*, 10, 2, 193-207.

Weber, M. (1949). *The methodology of the social sciences*. New York: Free Press.

Werner, E. E. (2003). Protective Factors and Individual Resilience. In J. P. Shonkoff & S. J. Meisels (Eds.), *Handbook of Early Childhood Intervention*. 2nd Edition. (pp. 115-132). Cambridge: Cambridge University Press.

Wilkinson, R. & Marmot, M. (2003). Introduction. In World Health Organization (WHO). *The Solid Facts*. 2nd Edition (edited by R. Wilkinson & M. Marmot). (pp. 7-9). Europe: World Health Organization.

Winther-Jensen, T. (2011). Educational Borrowing: A Model and the Genesis of Danish Social Pedagogy. In, J. Kornbeck & N. Rosendal Jensen (Eds.), *Social Pedagogy for the Entire Lifespan*, Volume I (pp. 51-64). Bremen: Europäischer Hochschulverlag.

World Health Organization (WHO). (2003). *The Solid Facts*. 2nd Edition (edited by R. Wilkinson & M. Marmot). Europe: World Health Organization.

Xenakis, N. & Goldberg, J.(2010). The Young Women's Program: A health and wellness model to empower adolescents with physical disabilities, *Disability and Health Journal*, *3*, 2, 125-129.

Young, I. M. (2011). *Responsibility for Justice*. Oxford: Oxford University Press.

Zawadski, B., cited by Allport G. W. (1979). *The Nature of Prejudice*. New York: Basic Books, p. 87.

About the Author

Paul Stephens, a Briton in Norway, is Inaugural Professor of Social Pedagogy at the University of Stavanger. He was awarded a B.Sc. (Hons) and a PhD in Sociology at the University of London. His aim in this book is to make Social Pedagogy much better known and understood in the UK and in other parts of the English-Speaking world.